# And The GRAMMY® Goes To...

## The Official Story Of Music's Most Coveted Award

*David Wild*
*Foreword by Quincy Jones*

NATIONAL ACADEMY OF RECORDING ARTS & SCIENCES®

This edition is published by State Street Press
by special arrangement with
Ann Arbor Media Group LLC
2500 South State Street
Ann Arbor, MI  48104

Printed and bound in Canada.

Library of Congress Cataloging-in-Publication Data on file.

ISBN-13: 978-0-681-49739-9
ISBN-10: 0-681-49739-4

Book Design by Danny Nanos and Photo Retouching by George Nanos.

Grammy and the gramophone logo are registered trademarks of
The Recording Academy and are used under license.

Printed on chlorine free paper made with 10% post-consumer waste

# Foreword

## Quincy Jones

A half century ago when a small group of us in the music business came together, we honestly had absolutely no idea where it would lead. We had come together with the idea of creating an organization designed to help promote and strengthen the music business—or the phonograph industry, as it was then sometimes known—as well as recognize the cultural importance of the recorded arts, and perhaps even start an annual awards dinner celebrating excellence as our associates in the film and television businesses had already done.

Now—some 50 years later—it's clear that what we started way back then was something very special indeed—the National Academy of Recording Arts & Sciences, and within a year or so, the Grammy Awards themselves. And so it is that the remarkable events that have followed over this past half century at the Grammy Awards—now documented in this fine book—represent a dream come true and *then* some.

Today, The Recording Academy is involved in a truly extraordinary range of musical, educational, and charitable activities. And at a time when our music business—and our musical world—continues to change and evolve in very dramatic ways, it's clear to me that we need an organization like The Academy more than ever, fighting for our music and our musicians, just as we need the Grammys to put its powerful global spotlight on many of our finest recording artists.

The Grammy Awards have quite rightly come to be called "Music's Biggest Night." Trust me, it doesn't get any bigger or better than the Grammys. And let me tell you from personal experience, winning a Grammy award is a tremendous, sometimes even overwhelming thrill. Beyond all the lights, cameras, and action of Grammy night, that shining award itself remains the ultimate accolade and symbol of respect from your creative colleagues. I've been told that I am the most nominated artist of all time, and that's a wonderful honor, although that doesn't diminish my desire to be nominated again in the future, and hopefully win a few more, too. Of course, it should be noted that having been nominated 79 times and having won 27 also means that I have the less sought after distinction of having the record for most Grammy losses.

Truth be told, I've had so many great Grammy nights to remember. Winning my first Grammy in 1963 for Best Instrumental Arrangement for the Count Basie Orchestra's "I Can't Stop Loving You" meant so much to me. Accepting several Grammys for my great friend Lena Horne and a few for myself for *The Dude* album in the early '80s was a great honor. A few years later there were those stunning Grammy nights celebrating my work with Michael Jackson and "We Are the World." Then there was the great honor of being presented with the Grammy Legend Award in 1991. My most recent Grammy was in 2001 for Best Spoken Word Album for *Q: The Autobiography of Quincy Jones*—meaning I finally found a way to win a Grammy for being "non-musical."

In the end, however, the Grammys are not about winning or losing, but about those singular musical moments. Standing at Staples Center and conducting for Alicia Keys and Jamie Foxx's tribute to my beloved late great friend Ray Charles a few years back, for instance, is something that I'll never forget— one of those many classic Grammy moments that I suspect will live forever. Just as importantly, there's that feeling backstage at a Grammy show with musicians of every sort pulling together to make "Music's Biggest Night" as big, beautiful, and memorable as it can possibly be.

Having traveled the world as much as I have, I've seen in countless ways that music really is our universal language. At their best, the Grammy Awards speak that language with an eloquence and elegance that unites us all.

My friend and mentor Frank Sinatra— another artist involved with the Grammys right from the beginning along with Nat "King" Cole and so many other of our musical greats—used to tell his audiences, "May you all live to be 100, and may the last voice you hear be mine." I won't borrow the Chairman's material here, but let me simply say it's been an honor to be associated with The Academy and the Grammys for these past 50 years and to see them grow and thrive and come to mean even more than we ever imagined.

Here's to the next 50 years.

# Preface

## Neil Portnow
*President/CEO, The Recording Academy*

*How do you* reflect the sound of 50 years of pop culture in a book? How do you portray the indelible images of the last five decades of television's—and perhaps the world's—defining musical performances on the printed page?

Well, if a picture is worth a thousand words and music is a universal language, then these pages contain a virtually endless collection of Grammy Awards stories from the last half century, and even give you a taste of what's to come in the next 50 years. Our story is the story of everyone from the Beatles to the Beastie Boys, Aretha Franklin to Kirk Franklin, Roger Miller to Faith Hill, Yo-Yo Ma to Sumi Jo, and a Count (Basie) to a Duke (Ellington).

For many, it's hard to remember a time without the Grammy Awards. The show literally launched the music awards telecast as we know it (it's no coincidence we call the Grammys "Music's Biggest Night"), and

the Grammys have maintained its status as not only the most respected music awards telecast, but also as the host of many of TV's and music's most memorable and unexpected live performances.

When The Recording Academy was formed in 1957, it was with the idea that music needed an artist-oriented organization: one that would honor not just stars, but also the producers, engineers, songwriters, and others who contributed so much to our culture, and one that would ultimately become the collective voice of all music people.

Since then, of course, the Grammy Awards has become synonymous with achievement in music. Whether it's a press release coming from an artist's media team or an obituary noting the passing of a musical giant, "Grammy winning" or "Grammy nominated" has become the universal catchphrase of musical accomplishment.

In our early years, legends such as Nat

"King" Cole, Quincy Jones, and Frank Sinatra helped lay the groundwork for our future. Today, legends-to-be look to the Grammy Awards to stage historic, one-of-a-kind performances. In between, fans around the world look to the Grammys to help them fully experience the quickly evolving music around them. And in the extremely fragmented pop culture of the future, the Grammy Awards will hold even greater importance for fans wrestling with a world where music emerges not just from big concert halls and major recording companies, but also from remote cultures and small bedrooms.

In these pages, you'll read about and see images from 49 years of amazing Grammy shows. We'll take you back to the late '50s and early '60s when pop was king, and through the early '80s when there was a King of Pop to the early '70s when fashions included green tuxes, vest-dresses, and ruffled blouses (for the men, of course), and the first part of the 21st century, when just about anything goes.

Along the way, though, there was always the music: traditional pop, funky R&B, country when it was known as country & western, classical, rock in all its variations, jazz, rap, gospel, folk, blues, and, yes, even to this day, polka. The Academy's voting members continue to honor them all in our myriad of categories that recognize all music, often from the very unique perspective of fellow music professionals, which results in decisions that aren't necessarily driven just by conventional wisdom or popular taste.

Of course, half the fun of being an awards show and music fan may be differing with the choices the Grammy voters make. After all, in a given year, it really *is* tough to choose an Album of the Year winner when the competition potentially includes Bruce Springsteen, OutKast, Bob Dylan, the Dixie Chicks, or U2. But we'll gladly stand up for our process because what we and our 18,000 members love most is creating awareness, helping boost careers, focusing attention on deserving artists, and staging television's most unique and exciting three-and-a-half hours.

# Table of Contents

# And the Grammy Goes to...

## The Five Sweetest Words in Music

"At 50," George Orwell once wrote, "everybody has the face they deserve." As the Grammy Awards prepare to face the Big 5-0 in 2008, let it be said that Music's Biggest Night is proving 50 is the new ageless, looking awfully spry for a show that has reflected and even changed the face of our music world over the past half century.

During the current era of unprecedented challenge in the music business, the Grammys continue to be seen far and wide as the music show that truly matters. While the manner in which songs are bought and sold may be changing, the truth is that our very primal passion for music remains undiminished. And so the need for a singular occasion that fully celebrates that undying human passion remains a profoundly powerful one.

In other words, the Grammys are not—and never will be—just another awards show.

Though the single biggest annual event in music today, the Grammy Awards, like the organization behind it, The Recording Academy, had relatively humble beginnings—at least by the standards of an organization of which Frank Sinatra, Sammy Davis Jr., and Dean Martin (virtually the entire Rat Pack), not to mention Nat "King" Cole and Quincy Jones were early members or proponents. Born at a 1957 meeting of music executives who felt that, like the film and TV industries, the music business also needed a platform to honor its craft, The Academy and the Grammys grew organically: first without a TV show, then with a taped special, and finally, in 1971, with the launch of what has become music's definitive live annual broadcast worldwide.

Having been fortunate enough to have worked on the Grammy Awards telecast as a writer for

*Left page: CBS Entertainment gathered many past Grammy winners together for this historic photo session in January 1983 at CBS Television City in Los Angeles to celebrate the Grammys' 25th anniversary Row 1: Michelle Phillips (Mamas and the Papas), Dionne Warwick, Helen Reddy, Stephanie Mills, Tommy Chong, Cheech Marin Row 2: Rita Moreno, Tim Hauser and Cheryl Bentyne (Manhattan Transfer), Andrae Crouch, Glen Campbell Row 3: Alan Paul (Manhattan Transfer), William Guest (Pips), Gladys Knight, Edward Patten and Bubba Knight (Pips), Harry Nilsson Row 4: B.B. King, Richard Carpenter, Karen Carpenter, Debby Boone, Johnny Rivers Row 5: Daryl Dragon, Toni Tennille, Dick Van Dyke, Henry Mancini, Steve Allen, Lalo Schifrin, Burt Bacharach This page: Frank Sinatra presents at the first Grammy dinner*

nearly a decade now, I feel as though I have been a most privileged witness to some of the many ways in which Music's Biggest Night has continued to grow and evolve during its recent past. At the same time, to look back at all of the history that brought us to this special point in time—which this book does so colorfully—is to recognize that change really has been one of the constants at the Grammy Awards.

"From the very beginning, the Grammys were always meant to change with the times," says Christine Farnon, the former executive vice president of The Recording Academy, who herself played an important part in putting together the Grammy Awards from the very start. "To watch the show, and The Recording Academy, change and grow over the years and become everything that they are today has been the fulfillment of a very big dream."

Pierre Cossette—the man who did so much to transform the Grammys into a live event and whose name became synonymous with the show in TV production circles—feels similarly today. "I like to think the Grammys matter because the Grammys are subject to change," says Cossette. "The beautiful truth is you never know what you're going to get on the Grammy show. Even *I* never knew."

Fortunately, at age 50, the Grammy Awards telecast also continues to matter to many of the finest and most enduring artists whose music has graced our lives during the past 50 years—as well as to the many men and women for whom bringing the show to life behind the scenes each year continues to be very much an act of musical passion.

"A Grammy means the measurement of the work that we do as artists, writers, composers, arrangers, producers as judged by our peers," says Stevie Wonder, who won the most recent of his 25 Grammy Awards during the 49th Annual Grammy show, when he shared an award with another all-time Grammy favorite, Tony Bennett. "It's a tremendous honor to be judged favorably by other people who listen very closely and decide how they feel. When you

**This page:** *Grammy producer Pierre Cossette and first live Grammy telecast host Andy Williams*

feel the respect of your peers, it's still a stunning and exciting thing. I looked forward to the Grammys almost like it was Christmas. You don't always win, of course, so I don't take that personally. But I am very happy with the many blessings I have received at the Grammy Awards, and I love knowing that people enjoyed it when I have had the chance to perform with other people on the show."

As Wonder rightly points out, "Grammy night brings all sorts of people together. To let you know how credible the gift of music really is, I believe when you hear bluegrass played next to hip-hop, gospel or the blues or rock or jazz or classical or pop on Grammy night, that's the closest that we all come as humans. For me, the Grammys are really about the whole spectrum of expression. And that's what is so exciting to me—that the Grammys have become a statement calling out that when we all come together, we really *can* be a united world."

"The greatest thing that ever happened to me is to be in the Grammy category of Best Traditional Pop Vocal," adds Tony Bennett. "This category has been the premise of my musical career, which celebrates the

best popular music ever created in the world—and has allowed me to win 14 Grammy Awards and a Lifetime Achievement Award, which I treasure. Attending the Grammys once a year and seeing all of the top musical artists in the world is a thrill of a lifetime for me."

Aretha Franklin—the Queen of Soul herself and a 17-time Grammy winner—explains that for her, "The Grammys are a symbol and musical standard that every artist should aspire to—to the level of this most coveted and most prestigious award. I reach for excellence in music, and the Grammy is a barometer and a sure confirmation that I am doing my best work and that it is appreciated by The Academy, my colleagues and peers, as they are the final voters. It is most fulfilling and rewarding to receive a Grammy, to say the least."

Indeed, the Grammy Awards' long-standing mission of celebrating musical excellence in all areas clearly touches a nerve with many of music's finest all across the musical landscape.

"The Grammys to me embody all things musical regardless of genre," says Vince Gill, who won his 18th Grammy Award at the 49th annual show. "And

**This page:** *Aretha Franklin with the Righteous Brothers at the 17th Grammys*

to be regarded as musical, it's the whole reason I ever picked up an instrument."

Artists like Bonnie Raitt acknowledge the pure power the Grammy can have on one's career. "Being honored by my peers at the Grammys has brought so much validation, not only for me personally, but for so many roots and non-mainstream artists that struggle for wider recognition. That night in 1990, when I won for *Nick of Time*, literally changed my life," she says, referencing one of the Grammy's most poignant moments of impact.

And for U2 guitarist The Edge, the Grammy is the ultimate symbol of artistic achievement. "There are few enough times when you get a glimpse of how your work has gone down with the rock and roll cognoscenti," he says. "Nothing gives you this better than seeing how your record does at the Grammys. A nomination is a fine thing but to win a Grammy is an amazing feeling. It never gets old; you never take it for granted. Peer approval is a real blessing."

For Carlos Santana—who famously won a record-tying eight awards during the 42nd show for his *Supernatural* comeback—the Grammys have a significance that seems almost supernatural itself. "The Grammys are supremely important because they take time to validate the contributions of songwriters and musicians who give birth to songs that raise consciousness and make an everlasting impression on life, people, and the planet," says the internationally beloved guitar god.

This page: *Vince Gill at the 41st Grammys • The Edge at the 46th Grammys with Bruce Springsteen and Elvis Costello*

And while music is always at the heart of the Grammy experience, over all these decades on television, the Grammys have managed to have their impact in another medium as well.

According to Leslie Moonves, CEO of the CBS Corporation, "Over the past half century, the show has managed to make not simply music history, but television history as well. The enduring success and tremendous impact of the Grammy show are a testament not just to the power of great music but also to true broadcasting in the very best sense of the word. Year after year, the show delivers both great music and compelling television, as well as the sort of unique performances and musical events that you can only see on the Grammys, whether it's the reunion of Simon & Garfunkel, Prince and Beyoncé performing together for the first time, or the Police going back on the beat at the beginning of last year's show. We are extremely proud that CBS has been the television home for the Grammys for virtually its entire illustrious history as a live event, and we look forward to making much more history together with The Recording Academy in the years to come."

According to co-executive producer Ken Ehrlich, making history at the Grammy Awards show comes with the territory as many of the now legendary "Grammy moments"—uniquely staged performances and unexpected pairings of artists—continue to prove. "Television used to be a place where watercooler

moments actually *meant* something," says Ehrlich, "but it's become more difficult to create those moments due to the availability of so many other entertainment options and platforms for viewers to consider. Fortunately, event television—and the Grammys in particular—remains one of the only places where it's important for viewers to be out there watching live rather than just catching it later online or on TiVo. The show marks a time each year when a majority of music fans and others can all discover something at the same time."

Of course, for the Grammys to be great event

**This page:** *Carlos Santana enjoying eight wins at the 42nd Grammys*

television, it helps if the show is a real event. "We go into each Grammy show wanting to reflect the music of the past year, but also with a mandate for once-in-a-lifetime moments that can help launch careers or reinvigorate careers and help viewers share a sense of discovery," Ehrlich explains. "I think there isn't a time when we finish a show and somebody doesn't inevitably come up and say, 'How are you going to top *that* next year?' We take that as the gauntlet being thrown down. Anything less would be boring to us and to the audience, and we always want to remain vital and exciting for the viewers."

The Grammys take the big chances on a very big level. As co-executive producer John Cossette—who as Pierre Cossette's son literally grew up with the show—points out, "The Grammy Awards are big in every way, and they've only gotten bigger in size and in ambition. I had just turned 14 at the time of the first live Grammy show. So I've seen the Grammys go from a show with dinner tables at the Hollywood Palladium and my father sending me and a few of my friends out onto Sunset Boulevard trying to pull in enough people

to fill the place, to a show where we are turning away people at Staples Center. That's *quite* a leap."

And so at age 50, how big are the Grammys exactly? According to John Cossette, "To put it all in perspective in terms of size and scope, on show day we have 23 stage managers and we're catering for 1,500 people. The largest Broadway show you will attend will have four. Our running crew of stage-hands and technicians is approximately 300; a Broadway show or an arena is about 60. We have over 900 computer-ized lights, and hang over 300,000 pounds from the ceiling of Staples Center. That's quite an incredible operation for an annual show. But all the effort is worth it because the show matters to people."

Ultimately, the reasons why the Grammys mat-ter—and just how they matter—vary from person to person. For director Walter Miller who's been calling the shots for years, ultimately it's the grandeur. "I think that the Grammys became Music's Biggest Night by including a little of everything. It's the diversity and the quality of the music that's made this

This page: *Bonnie Raitt and producer Phil Ramone at the 47th Grammys*

the top night of music—the musical equivalent of the Academy Awards."

Such standing, however, does not come without a lot of hard work. "As a result of what we do and all the personalities that must be dealt with, the Grammys are probably the most challenging event in live television," Miller adds, "and we all still love to deal with that challenge. The show is always about the artists, and they almost always rise to the occasion. I think for a lot of people, the Grammys are a pinnacle moment. The show is still something special because many people feel when they've appeared on the Grammys, that means that they have *truly* arrived."

Phil Ramone, a 13-time Grammy winner himself and a longtime member of the Academy's television committee, confirms as much. "I think when your passion and your love is music and recording, there are certain moments of recognition that you will *never* forget," says the legendary music producer. "When you have your first hit and hear your music on the radio and see it on the charts, that's an incredible feeling. But right about then you start to pray that

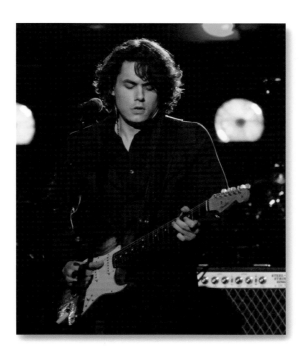

somebody nominates that piece of music to become a Grammy for you. Because a Grammy award, well, that's what you show your children. A Grammy is one of those things that mean you're not a secret anymore."

At 50, the Grammy awards are a non-secret worth keeping. And for artists of every generation, the non-secret is out. "The Grammy serves as a powerful focal point for the hopes and dreams of musicians," says John Mayer, who has won five Grammys in the last five years. "Whether recording your first demo in your garage, or your fourth major label album in a large studio, winning a Grammy is a dream that pushes music artists to the edge of their abilities and beyond."

As the book you now hold before you clearly suggests, at age 50, the Grammy Awards have in fact already seen a great deal—the good, the great, and even the occasional ugly. Yet let there be no doubt that as long as there is a song somewhere in our collective heart, there is much left for all of us still to see and, of course, so much still to hear.

By all means, let's all stay tuned.

**This page:** *John Mayer performs at the 49th Grammys*

# 1950s

The '50s gave the world the hula hoop, the Cold War, hot jazz, McCarthyism, the Suez Crisis, *Peyton Place, The Catcher in the Rye,* rock and roll, and, by decade's end, the Grammy Awards too with the formation of the National Academy of Recording Arts & Sciences. Right from the start, the Grammy Awards inevitably and intriguingly reflected a world in transition, musically and otherwise, with winners at the 1st Annual Grammy Awards— announced on May 4, 1959—ranging from "Tom Dooley" to "Tequila" and Van Cliburn to the Chipmunks.

# 1960s

"The '60s were when hallucinogenic drugs were really, really big," eventual Grammy host Ellen DeGeneres once noted of the first full decade of the Grammy Awards. "And I don't think it's a coincidence that we had the type of shows we had then, like *The Flying Nun*." If you were there and you still remember the '60s, you might recall a series of television specials called "The Best on Record" that celebrated some of the many Grammy winners in a decade that brought us the Beatles, the U.S. space program, JFK and LBJ, Martin Luther King Jr., the Peace Corps, American troops in Vietnam, Woodstock, Altamont, Betty Friedan's *The Feminine Mystique*, and the pill.

# 1st Annual Grammy Awards

AWARDS DINNERS HELD IN LOS ANGELES AND NEW YORK

*Eligibility Year: January 1, 1958–December 31, 1958*
*Announced on May 4, 1959*

*In the beginning,* there was heaven and earth and the 1st Annual Grammy Awards—more or less in that order.

On May 4, 1959, many of music's elite—including Frank Sinatra, Sammy Davis Jr., Dean Martin, Gene Autry, Johnny Mercer, Henry Mancini, and André Previn—gathered for a black-tie dinner and awards presentation inside the Grand Ballroom of the Beverly Hilton. At the same time, other new Academy members were gathering at a function held simultaneously in New York City. "The Grammy Awards were a formal event from the beginning and very much in keeping with the times," says Christine Farnon, who was instrumental in organizing the first show and would go on to become The Academy's Executive Vice President. "As I recall, no one objected to dressing black-tie

back then, though like so much else, that would change eventually."

But this Grammy night, and several to follow, was held in hotel ballrooms on both coasts. The Los Angeles event was emceed by popular political comedian Mort Sahl and featured a musical sketch titled "How South Was My Pacific." The night was by numerous accounts a significant success. *Billboard*—then actually still called *The Billboard*—ran its account of the first night of Music's Biggest Night with a headline declaring that "Academy Smoothly Moves Into Orbit: First Awards Well-Organized Affair As Top Stars Go On Parade." The trade magazine even favorably compared the Grammys' debut to the far more established Oscars and Emmys: "It sharply contrasted similar affairs staged by the two older

Left page: *Dean Martin and Sammy Davis Jr.* • *Johnny Mercer and Henry Mancini*
This page: *Peggy Lee, Record of the Year nominee for "Fever"*

**WINNER SNAPSHOT**
**Record of the Year**
"Nel Blu Dipinto Di Blu (Volare)" • Domenico Modugno
**Album of the Year**
*The Music from Peter Gunn* • Henry Mancini
**Song of the Year**
"Nel Blu Dipinto Di Blu (Volare)" • Domenico Modugno, songwriter

entertainment academies in its precision-like pace in handling the presentations."

As well organized as the night may have been, from the very start, there would be surprises on Grammy night. While Sinatra led all nominees with a grand total of six nominations, he would not turn out to be the night's biggest winner. Rather, the very first Record of the Year and Song of the Year awards both went to "Nel Blu Dipinto Di Blu (Volare)" by Domenico Modugno, while Album of the Year went to *The Music from Peter Gunn* by Henry Mancini.

As for Sinatra, he fortunately didn't go home empty-handed. He won his first Grammy not for singing, but rather as art director for his *Only the Lonely* album that won Best Album Cover. And though only 28 categories were presented on this first Grammy night—the least ever—the first winners suggested the diversity that would come to mark the Grammy Awards, with winners that ranged from Ella Fitzgerald (Best Vocal Performance, Female, and Best Jazz Performance, Individual) to David Seville and the Chipmunks (Best Comedy Performance and Best Recording for Children, while Best Engineered Record, Non Classical went to Ted Keep for "The Chipmunk Song"), from the Kingston Trio's "Tom Dooley" (Best County & Western Performance) to the Champs' "Tequila" (Best Rhythm & Blues Performance).

Much more—in every conceivable way, and some ways still inconceivable—was still to come.

**Left page:** *Henry Mancini, Julie London, and André Previn • Ross Bagdasarian, creator of David Seville and the Chipmunks*
**This page:** *Mort Sahl*

*Did You Know ...? Although it does not win, "The Chipmunk Song" becomes the only children's or comedy recording to be nominated in Record of the Year. • The Everly Brothers compete with themselves when they are nominated for "All I Have to Do Is Dream" and "Bird Dog" in Best Country & Western Performance. They lose to "Tom Dooley" by the Kingston Trio. • Domenico Modugno's wins for "Nel Blu Dipinto Di Blu (Volare)" in Record of the Year and Song of the Year mark the only time a foreign language recording has won in these categories.*

# 2nd Annual Grammy Awards

*Eligibility Year: January 1, 1959–August 31, 1959*
*Announced on November 29, 1959*

*The first* thing you should know about the 2nd Annual Grammy Awards is that they weren't actually "annual" at all. In fact, this awards presentation marked the only time in Grammy history that two awards presentations were ever made in one year, with both the 1st and 2nd Grammys falling in 1959. Call it a slightly embarrassing case of premature validation.

The 2nd Grammys did, however, mark another first: the first Grammys to be presented on television as a taped "NBC Sunday Showcase," which aired on November 29, 1959. Hosted by Meredith Willson—who wrote the Broadway show *The Music Man*—the television program offered performances by classical pianist Van Cliburn, comedian Shelley Berman, Nat "King" Cole, Bobby Darin, folk singer Jimmy Driftwood,

Duke Ellington, Ella Fitzgerald, trumpeter Jonah Jones, the Kingston Trio, and the Mormon Tabernacle Choir. Say this for the Grammys—it always had range.

The award winners themselves were announced at private dinner ceremonies held in Los Angeles and New York. Following the awards presentations, the audience watched the broadcast of the first Grammy special. With the '60s about to get underway and the times about to start a-changing, Darin and Frank Sinatra emerged as the big winners. Darin was named Best New Artist of 1959—the first winner in that category—and he also won Record of the Year with his timeless version of "Mack the Knife." Sinatra took Album of the Year for *Come Dance with Me* and Best Vocal

*Left page: Jonah Jones*
*This page: Meredith Willson and Van Cliburn*

**WINNER SNAPSHOT**
**Record of the Year**
"Mack the Knife" • Bobby Darin
**Album of the Year**
*Come Dance with Me* • Frank Sinatra
**Song of the Year**
"The Battle of New Orleans" • Jimmy Driftwood, songwriter
**Best New Artist**
Bobby Darin

Performance, Male, for its title track (which also won Billy May a Grammy for Best Arrangement).

Other winners included Jonah Jones' Best Jazz Performance, Group, award for his very '50s album *I Dig Chicks*, poet Carl Sandburg for narrating *A Lincoln Portrait*, and the iconic Ethel Merman for Best Broadway Show Album for *Gypsy*, which tied with Gwen Verdon for *Redhead*.

For all that, even in its earliest TV incarnation, there was never a shortage of critics both willing and able to take their shots at the young if not innocent Grammy show. Writing in the *New York World Telegram*, Harriet Von Horne noted, "But ... the pandering to the primitive, uninformed taste that mars so much of TV fare, was on view here ... Here was a costly show, brilliantly produced ... and it had the whole range of music to choose from. So we had a reading by Shelley Berman instead of Carl Sandburg. We had the clanging, twanging Kingston Trio when we might have had Ethel Merman ..."

Others were more understanding, even supportive. *Variety* said, "Grammy Makes Good in TV Bow" in a front-page banner headline, and the *Hollywood Reporter* announced "Grammy Telecast Cut Above Average Award Programs."

Through the good, the bad, and the ugly, there would be many more cuts and many more kudos in the years to come.

*Left page from top: Jonah Jones, Meredith Willson, Jimmy Driftwood, Bobby Darin, and Shelley Berman with the Mormon Tabernacle Choir • Jimmy Driftwood*
*This page: Meredith Willson and Bobby Darin • Meredith Willson and Shelley Berman, who won Best Comedy Performance, Spoken Word*

*Did You Know ...?* Nat "King" Cole's "Midnight Flyer" wins Best Performance by a "Top 40" Artist over nominees Elvis Presley, Sarah Vaughan, the Coasters, Floyd Robinson, and Neil Sedaka. This is Cole's only win; he received a Lifetime Achievement Award in 1990 and has five recordings in the Grammy Hall of Fame: "(Get Your Kicks On) Route 66," "Mona Lisa," "Nature Boy," "Unforgettable," and "The Christmas Song." • Elvis Presley has his first nominations, but no wins. He is nominated for "A Fool Such As I" in Record of the Year and for "A Big Hunk of Love" in Best Performance by a "Top 40" Artist and in Best Rhythm & Blues Performance. He loses to Bobby Darin in Record of the Year, Nat "King" Cole in "Top 40," and Dinah Washington in Best Rhythm & Blues Performance.

# 3rd Annual Grammy Awards

AWARDS DINNERS HELD IN LOS ANGELES AND NEW YORK

*Eligibility Year: September 1, 1959–November 30, 1960*
*Announced on April 12, 1961*

*For the* next two years, the Grammy revolution would not be televised.

Both the 3rd and 4th Annual Grammy Awards presentations were made only at private dinner ceremonies, with no television component. As difficult as it may be to imagine today, the still young Recording Academy was making its case to the big three networks that a music awards show belonged on their crowded schedules.

Meanwhile, awards were handed out at dinners in Recording Academy chapter cities Los Angeles

(the Crystal Ballroom of the Beverly Hills Hotel with Mort Sahl in a return engagement as emcee) and New York (in the main ballroom at the Hotel Astor at Times Square) with entertainment in Los Angeles provided by jazz acts the Gene Rains Combo, Pete Jolly Trio, and the Skeets Herfurt Group.

In what could be viewed as a Genius move, Ray Charles emerged the big winner, earning his first ever Grammys based on his groundbreaking and now classic album *The Genius of Ray Charles*. Brother Ray's album won Best Vocal Performance Album, Male, while "Georgia on My Mind" won Best Vocal Performance Single Record or Track, Male, and Best Performance by a Pop Single Artist. Charles' fourth award was for "Let the Good Times Roll" for Best Rhythm & Blues Performance.

The good times also rolled on Grammy night for comedian Bob Newhart. *The Button-Down Mind of Bob Newhart* became the first comedy set to win Album of the Year. The future sitcom icon also took Best New Artist of 1960 and Best Comedy Performance, Spoken Word, for *The Button-Down Mind Strikes Back!* Percy Faith's instrumental gem "Theme from a Summer Place," meanwhile, took Record of the Year.

The great Ella Fitzgerald—a Grammy winner in

*Left page: Bobby Darin, Mort Sahl, Henry Mancini and Giselle McKenzie at the Los Angeles awards dinner*
*This page: Songwriter Jimmy McHugh, Mort Sahl, Louella Parsons and Peggy Lee congratulate Marvin Schwartz on his win for Best Album Cover for* Latin A La Lee

**WINNER SNAPSHOT**
**Record of the Year**
"Theme from a Summer Place" • Percy Faith
**Album of the Year**
*The Button-Down Mind of Bob Newhart* • Bob Newhart
**Song of the Year**
"Theme from Exodus" • Ernest Gold, songwriter
**Best New Artist**
Bob Newhart

each of the first two Grammy presentations—won a pair of awards for her album *Mack the Knife—Ella in Berlin* and its title track. Henry Mancini also added to his growing collection with three more Grammys, including two for work on the soundtrack of *Mr. Lucky*, a Blake Edwards–produced television series of the time.

Other awards included opera star Leontyne Price's first Grammy for Best Classical Performance—Vocal Soloist (*A Program of Song—Leontyne Price Recital*), Marty Robbins for Best Country & Western Performance ("El Paso"), Harry Belafonte's first Grammy for Best Performance—Folk (*Swing Dat Hammer*, a record built around African-American chain gang chants), and Gil Evans and Miles Davis for *Sketches of Spain* in a category with a name that future Grammy sponsor Timex would love: Best Jazz Composition of More Than Five Minutes Duration.

In 1960 The Recording Academy also formally adopted its official credo, penned by early Academy booster and all-around satirist Stan Freberg. His credo was quite serious about The Academy's goals, in a Preamble to the Constitution kind of way:

*We, the National Academy of Recording Arts & Sciences, being dedicated to the advancement of the phonograph record, do pledge ourselves as follows:*

*We shall judge a record on the basis of sheer artistry, and artistry alone—artistry in writing, performance, musicianship and engineering.*

*A record shall, in the opinion of The Academy, either attain the highest degree of excellence possible in the category entered, or it shall not receive an Academy Award. Sales and mass popularity are the yardsticks of the record business. They are not the yardsticks of this Academy.*

*We are concerned here with the phonograph record as an art form. If the record industry is to grow, not decline in stature, if it is to foster a greater striving for excellence in its own field, if it is to discourage mediocrity and encourage greatness, we, as its spokesmen, can accept no other Credo.*

Clearly, not Freberg's funniest work by a long shot, but words to live by nonetheless.

*Left page: Gogi Grant presents Jo Stafford and Paul Weston with the Best Comedy Performance (Musical) Grammy for Jonathan and Darlene Edwards in Paris • Benny Carter and Peggy Lee present Luis P. (Val) Valentin with the Best Engineering Contribution, Popular Recording, Grammy for Ella Fitzgerald Sings the George and Ira Gershwin Songbook This page: Singer Dotty Wayne, composer Ray Rasch, and engineer Hugh Davies*

# 4th Annual Grammy Awards

## AWARDS DINNERS HELD IN CHICAGO, LOS ANGELES, AND NEW YORK

### Eligibility Year: December 1, 1960–November 30, 1961
### Announced on May 29, 1962

*D*uring the eligibility year for the 4th Annual Grammy Awards, the Vietnam War officially began, Dwight Eisenhower warned of the growing military industrial complex, John F. Kennedy was sworn in as president, a chimp named Ham was launched into space, the U.S. military invaded Cuba's Bay of Pigs, Roger Maris hit 61 home runs, and a young singer/songwriter born Robert Zimmerman moved to New York to become Bob Dylan.

Yet in pure Grammy terms, the most significant event of the year may have been Judy Garland's legendary comeback at New York's Carnegie Hall. *Judy at Carnegie Hall*, the resulting live album, earned Grammy awards for Album of the Year (Other Than Classical); Best Solo Vocal Performance, Female; Best Engineering Contribution, Popular Recording, for engineer Robert Arnold; and Best Album Cover (Other Than Classical) for art director Jim Silke.

The 4th Annual Grammy Awards also marked the biggest Grammy year ever for a man who was already becoming a Grammy institution in his own right—Henry Mancini. Mancini's wins at these festivities were sparked primarily by the huge success of his music for the Audrey Hepburn smash *Breakfast at Tiffany's*. "Moon River" (which also won the best song Oscar) won the Grammy for Record of the Year, Song of the Year, and Best Arrangement, while the title track won Best Performance by an Orchestra, For Other Than Dancing, and the sound track was victorious for Best Sound Track Album or Recording of Score from Motion Picture or Television. Ever the gentleman, Mancini did not refuse the

**WINNER SNAPSHOT**
**Record of the Year**
"Moon River" • Henry Mancini
**Album of the Year (Other Than Classical)**
*Judy at Carnegie Hall* • Judy Garland
**Song of the Year**
"Moon River" • Henry Mancini & Johnny Mercer, songwriters
**Best New Artist**
Peter Nero

awards because of their overly wordy titles.

This Grammy year also saw the emergence of comedy team Mike Nichols and Elaine May, who won the Best Comedy Performance award (for *An Evening with Mike Nichols and Elaine May*). Nichols would later go on to even further prominence as a film director, starting with *Who's Afraid of Virginia Woolf* (1966) and *The Graduate* (1967).

Choral conductor Robert Shaw won the first of what would be 16 Grammy Awards over the years, earning Best Classical Performance, Choral (Other Than Opera), for *Bach: B Minor Mass*.

Also, by 1961, The Academy was beginning to act on a mission that was geared to make the organization not just the presenter of the Grammy Awards, but also one that sought to foster growth and dialog for its music-making members. A November 1961 Academy-sponsored panel discussion now seems like a quaint time capsule and found panelists debating the then pressing issue: "Is Stereo Necessary?" The panel included jazz greats Gerry Mulligan and Woody Herman as well as RCA chief engineer Bill Miltenberg and resulted in exchanges like the following (just substitute CD vs. MP3 to bring the dialog into the current day):

Miltenberg: *"I think of monaural recording ... like having a shower with the water coming from just one point. I like to take a shower with the water coming from all directions."*

Mulligan: *"Yeah, but you don't want the hot*

*water coming from one point and all the cold coming from another."*

The Grammys would not actually be broadcast in stereo for many years to come—though it's now available in 5.1 surround sound—yet the show itself was now growing bigger and, yes, hotter with every year.

Left page clockwise from top: *Jackie Cooper, Jo Stafford, Carl Reiner, and Johnny Mercer* • *Stan Freberg (left), Vic Damone (center), and guests at the Los Angeles awards dinner* This page: *André Previn*

# 5th Annual Grammy Awards

AWARDS DINNERS HELD IN CHICAGO, LOS ANGELES, AND NEW YORK

*Eligibility Year: December 1, 1961–November 30, 1962*
*Announced on May 15, 1963*
"The Best on Record" airs on December 8, 1963

*If you're* going to have somebody explain to the watching world exactly what your organization does, who better than the Chairman of the Board himself?

Starting with the 5th Annual Grammy Awards, the National Academy of Recording Arts & Sciences followed its nontelevised presentation ceremonies with the first of what would eventually be six NBC specials called "The Best on Record." The inaugural "The Best on Record" show—sponsored by Timex—began in high style with Frank Sinatra welcoming the viewer and promising that "for the next 60 minutes you're going to see the finest the record business has to offer." Sinatra's claim was backed up by the show's cast list that, in addition to himself, included everyone from Mahalia Jackson to Richard Rodgers, Dean Martin to comedian Bob Newhart, and Bing Crosby to the New Christy Minstrels.

Sinatra then went on to muse rather poetically about music and the mission of the Grammys. "You know, a record is a kind of a weird thing," said the man they called

The Voice. "It's just a slab with a little hole in it, and yet it can do almost anything for you. It can bring a symphony into your living room ... You can make bums out of the artists and artists out of the bums." Then showing off a shiny Grammy award, Sinatra added, "Now this is the pay-off—it's called a Grammy. They're voted once a year by the members of the National Academy of Recording Arts & Sciences, not for selling a million records mind you— you get *bread* for that—this is for contributions to the art of recording."

Setting the template for future "Best on Record" shows, a variety of the year's Grammy-winning musical acts and other performers was introduced by high-profile members of the music community, as well as other top stars, in a studio-based setting.

For instance, Bob Newhart—the Grammy winner as Best New Artist of 1960—performed a musically themed standup before introducing pianist Peter Nero, who won Best Performance by an Orchestra or Instrumentalist with Orchestra, Primarily Not Jazz or for Dancing (perhaps

Left page: *Connie Francis*
This page: *Frank Sinatra and Bing Crosby*

**WINNER SNAPSHOT**
**Record of the Year**
"I Left My Heart in San Francisco" • Tony Bennett
**Album of the Year (Other Than Classical)**
*The First Family* • Vaughn Meader
**Song of the Year**
"What Kind of Fool Am I?" • Leslie Bricusse & Anthony Newley, songwriters

**Best New Artist**
Robert Goulet

**SPECIAL MERIT AWARDS**
Golden Achievement Award
Bing Crosby
(Awarded in 1962 and presented on the 5th Grammy Awards)

obviously the longest named category in the history of the Grammys) for his album *The Colorful Peter Nero*. Andy Williams—who was soon to become a fixture at Grammy shows—introduced an excellent segment that found Henry Mancini, already an 11-time Grammy winner by now, performing an instrumental medley of three of his greatest compositions: "Moon River," "Baby Elephant Walk," and the *Peter Gunn* television show theme.

Comedian Bill Dana revealed that he had once been head writer for Tony Bennett's short-lived 1956 TV show before introducing the singer's characteristically subtle performance of "I Left My Heart in San Francisco"—which won Record of the Year and Best Solo Vocal Performance, Male, as well as a Best Background Arrangement Grammy for Marty Manning. The distinguished Broadway composer Richard Rodgers—whose *No Strings* won Best Original Cast Show Album—introduced that show's star Diahann Carroll, who sang two songs from the musical. Bandleader Les Brown introduced a rousing performance of "If I Had a Hammer" by Peter, Paul & Mary, who took home Grammys for both Best Performance by a Vocal Group and Best Folk Recording. And after slyly joking about having drunk "a glass of milk," Dean Martin charmingly introduced Connie Francis to sing a startlingly fine rendition of the winning Song of the Year, "What Kind of Fool Am I?" written by Leslie Bricusse and Anthony Newley.

Toward the end of the show, Sinatra returned to make

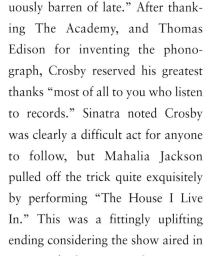

a historic presentation to Bing Crosby, first confessing, "We all stole from him." Sinatra explained that The Academy had voted unanimously to honor Crosby, a groundbreaking vocalist and recording artist, with a lifetime achievement award to be named after him. "Congratulations there, Bing, here's a little gold to add to your mint." Crosby accepted graciously, adding, "This is going to look very good on a mantel that has been conspicuously barren of late." After thanking The Academy, and Thomas Edison for inventing the phonograph, Crosby reserved his greatest thanks "most of all to you who listen to records." Sinatra noted Crosby was clearly a difficult act for anyone to follow, but Mahalia Jackson pulled off the trick quite exquisitely by performing "The House I Live In." This was a fittingly uplifting ending considering the show aired in the wake of the assassination of John F. Kennedy.

According to Ted Bergmann, the executive producer of "The Best on Record" specials, the airing of the first show was preempted in the aftermath of Kennedy's death. "NBC came to me and said, 'We'll schedule you for two weeks from now ... but you'll have to get Vaughn Meader off your show.'" Comedian and impersonator Meader had won Album of the Year (Other Than Classical) and Best Comedy Performance for his record of Kennedy-themed comedy, *The First Family*. In the wake of recent events, Meader's segment was quickly removed, and Tony Bennett was added to "The Best on Record" bill in his place.

*Left page clockwise from top left: Peter, Paul & Mary • Vaughn Meader • Bob Newhart • Dean Martin This page: Mahalia Jackson*

*Did You Know ...?* Joan Baez, George Jones, and Mel Tormé receive their first nominations. • Tony Bennett has his first nominations with two wins. He wins for "I Left My Heart in San Francisco" in Record of the Year and Best Solo Vocal Performance, Male. His album, I Left My Heart in San Francisco, is nominated in Album of the Year but loses to Vaughn Meader's The First Family. Bennett will go on to earn 14 wins over a period of 44 years. • Vladimir Horowitz has two wins; his first of 25 wins ending in 1992. He won for Columbia Records Presents Vladimir Horowitz in Album of the Year, Classical, and in Best Classical Performance, Soloist or Duo (Without Orchestra). • Georg Solti has his first nominations and win. He wins as conductor in Best Opera Recording for Verdi's Aida. He will go on to receive the most wins to date with 31 out of 74 nominations ending in 1998.

# 6th Annual Grammy Awards

AWARDS DINNERS HELD IN CHICAGO, LOS ANGELES, AND NEW YORK

*Eligibility Year: December 1, 1962–November 30, 1963*
*Announced on May 12, 1964*

*In a way,* the 6th Annual Grammy Awards was a victim of the Grammys' own success. The previous year's "The Best on Record" broadcast—a one-off production to test how well a televised music awards show would fair—was so widely watched that NBC, sponsor Timex, and The Recording Academy began negotiations for a long-term deal for an annual show. Like today, such complex deals involving multiple parties are not executed overnight. As a result, by the time this deal was hammered out, the 6th Grammy presentation had come and gone.

Yet despite the lack of TV presence, by the time of the 6th Annual Grammy Awards, the music industry's top honor had become established enough that the awards presentation was marked primarily by major awards going to both artists who had become Grammy favorites and fresh voices who were about to become legends.

On the established Grammy favorite side, Henry Mancini would win his 12th, 13th, and 14th Grammys during the presentation of the 6th Annual Grammys, all of them for the bittersweet "Days of Wine and Roses," which won both Record and Song of the Year as well as Best Background Arrangement. The film of the same name was a stark tale of alcohol addiction as told by the usually comedic director Blake Edwards and solidified one of the most productive director/composer partnerships of all time.

The freshest new voice came in the form of Album of the Year and Best Vocal Performance, Female, winner Barbra Streisand. Her solo debut, *The Barbra Streisand Album*, was recorded before she was 21 and set the stage for her remarkable run as a singer, actress, and stage performer.

*Left page: Tony Bennett and Jack Jones*
*This page: Grammy Awards table*

---

**WINNER SNAPSHOT**

**Record of the Year**
"Days of Wine and Roses" • Henry Mancini

**Album of the Year (Other Than Classical)**
*The Barbra Streisand Album* • Barbra Streisand

**Song of the Year**
"Days of Wine and Roses" • Henry Mancini & Johnny Mercer, songwriters

**Best New Artist**
Ward Swingle (The Swingle Singers)

Her Album of the Year win marked a turning point of sorts. Though Mancini would go on to win six more Grammys in the coming years, one of the albums Streisand beat was Andy Williams' *Days of Wine and Roses*, as well as the Singing Nun—stage name Soeur Sourire, real name Jeanine Deckers—who had a surprise hit with "Dominique," which *did* win for Best Gospel or Other Religious Recording (Musical), thank God.

Perhaps equally fresh was the first ever Grammy win for Quincy Jones, who took Best Instrumental Arrangement for Count Basie's "I Can't Stop Loving You." Jones would go on to win 26 more Grammys to date. In 2007, Jones commented that this first Grammy win remains "a true highlight" in one of music's most distinguished and enduring careers.

There were also awards (Best Vocal Performance, Male) for Jack Jones' now politically incorrect "Wives and Lovers," which included the lyrics "Hey little girl, comb your hair, fix your makeup / Soon he will open the door / Don't think because there's a ring on your finger / You needn't try anymore," and the relatively wholesome choice of a cappella classical vocal group Ward Swingle and the Swingle Singers for Best New Artist of 1963.

Yet there was at least one sign that the times were now truly a-changin', for both the Grammy Awards and the culture at large. Peter, Paul & Mary won two Grammys—Best Folk Recording and Best Performance by a Vocal Group—for their version of Dylan's classic "Blowin' in the Wind." And next year, four mop-topped Liverpudlians would emerge to take the Best New Artist award.

By the following year, the winds were blowin' the Grammys way, and Music's Biggest Night would be back on the air to stay.

Left page from top:
*Quincy Jones, Jack Jones, Steve Lawrence, Barbra Streisand, Eydie Gorme, Tony Bennett, and Count Basie at the New York awards dinner • Nino Tempo, April Stevens, Jayne Meadows, and Steve Allen at the Los Angeles awards dinner*
This page: *Vikki Carr at the Los Angeles awards dinner*

# 7th Annual Grammy Awards

On April 13, 1965, the British Invasion was officially complete.

While the 7th Annual Grammy Awards may not have constituted a complete surrender to the Beatles and their English fellow travelers, it didn't take long for the Grammys to acknowledge the stunning impact of the Fab Four following their American arrival in 1964. John, Paul, George, and Ringo themselves won two Grammy Awards—Best New Artist and Best Performance by a Vocal Group for "A Hard Day's Night." Furthermore, the group's wider cultural impact was also recognized indirectly when the Grammy for Best Engineered Recording, Special or Novel Effects, was presented to engineer Dave Hassinger for *The Chipmunks Sing the Beatles.*

"The Best on Record" television special for the year also reflected the Brave New Fab World

of 1964. After noting that the show was bringing together "the Great Society of the recording industry," Steve Allen explained at the start that this was a time in music when "it doesn't hurt if you're a Beatle or a Chipmunk or something like that. For people it's a little tougher." In fact, it wasn't hard to miss a certain anti-rock condescension creeping into the proceedings when Allen— who won the Best Original Jazz Composition for "Gravy Waltz" with Ray Brown the previous year— added, "Sometimes I put on the Rolling Stones just so I can turn them off."

The Stones did not win a Grammy or appear on "The Best on Record," but the Beatles memorably did. First, there was an introduction from famed Boston Pops Orchestra conductor Arthur Fiedler, who noted, "Until recently longhair has always been used as a term referring to classical music.

**WINNER SNAPSHOT**

**Record of the Year**
"The Girl from Ipanema" • Astrud Gilberto & Stan Getz

**Album of the Year**
*Getz/Gilberto* • Stan Getz & João Gilberto

**Song of the Year**
"Hello, Dolly!" • Jerry Herman, songwriter

**Best New Artist**
The Beatles

**SPECIAL MERIT AWARDS**

Bing Crosby Award
Frank Sinatra

Trustees Award
Phil Ramone

Lately it seems to have an entirely different meaning. The new longhairs have a new sound, a new beat, and, to say the least, very new haircuts." The show then cut to Twickenham Film Studios in London, where the Beatles were filming their second movie, *Help!* Peter Sellers—a favorite comic hero of the group—was at the studios to present the Fabs with their two Grammys, or as he called them, "Grandma Awards." Sellers and the boys proceeded to quip quite happily, before the Beatles broke into a slightly crazed version of the World War I standard "It's a Long Way to Tipperary." For the record, the Beatles did *not* sweep the rock awards—interestingly, the Best Rock & Roll Recording went to fellow Brit Petula Clark for "Downtown."

Certainly it wasn't all about rock and roll at the 7th Annual Grammy Awards. The bossa nova beat was still all the rage, with Record of the Year going to "The Girl from Ipanema" by Astrud Gilberto and Stan Getz and Album of the Year going to the *Getz/Gilberto* album by Stan Getz and João Gilberto. The Song of the Year

Grammy, meanwhile, went to Jerry Herman for "Hello, Dolly!" When Louis Armstrong had to cancel an appearance on "The Best on Record" at the last minute, producer George Schlatter and his team delivered an excellent late substitute to sing the song—Jimmy Durante. This was followed directly by an amusing appearance by Woody Allen, who had been nominated for Best Comedy Performance. "My wrists are completely healed," Allen explained of his loss to Bill Cosby (*I Started Out As a Child*). As Allen wryly noted, "It's a thrill for me to be included in this fantastic tribute being paid to the recording industry by the recording industry."

Speaking of fantastic tributes, this year's "The Best on Record" ended with one richly deserved salute to the late great Nat "King" Cole, who had died of lung cancer on February 15, 1965. Steve Allen returned to the screen to point out that Cole had been one of the founders and one of the first members of the Board of Governors of The Recording Academy. Sammy Davis Jr. then beautifully paid his respects to Cole by singing a medley of his unforgettable and timeless songs.

*Left page clockwise from top left: Roger Miller at the Nashville awards dinner • Jimmy Durante • Gary Owens (kneeling), Clark Burroughs, Sue Raney, Marilyn Burroughs, Nancy Wilson, and Donald O'Connor at the Los Angeles awards dinner*
*This page: Petula Clark*

*Did You Know ...?* Roger Miller has the most wins of the night with five Grammys including Best New Country & Western Artist. • The Beatles are the first group of the rock genre to win Best New Artist. • Marilyn Horne wins Most Promising New Classical Artist. • The Supremes earn their first nomination, for "Baby Love" in Best Rhythm & Blues Recording.

# 8th Annual Grammy Awards

AWARDS DINNERS HELD IN
CHICAGO, LOS ANGELES, NASHVILLE, AND NEW YORK

*Eligibility Year: December 1, 1964–November 1, 1965*
*Announced on March 15, 1966*
*"The Best on Record" airs on May 16, 1966*

As the Grammy Awards grew in influence and magnitude, they perhaps inevitably grew in controversy as well. As early as the 8th Annual Grammy Awards, signs were already appearing that, like all awards shows, the Grammys could never please everyone. A February 23, 1966, *Variety* article headlined "Razzberries for Grammys" took The Academy to task for slighting the R&B world in favor of country and western, and for overlooking Bob Dylan, "the single most influential figure in the pop field since Elvis Presley." In his March 7, 1966, commentary on the Grammys in the *Los Angeles Times*, Charles Champlin reported on both slights and noted "among the 218 final nominations in the 47 categories there is nary a single one any place for Bob Dylan ... The electric-haired poet-composer-performer of 'Tambourine Man' and a satchel-full of other recording successes, has to be counted one of the most influential as well as one of the biggest money-spinning talents to emerge big in 1965." When you consider the fact that among those other 1965 recording successes in Dylan's satchel was a little something called "Like a Rolling Stone," it's hard to argue even all these years later.

In the post-Beatles and Dylan era, the musical and generational range within the pop and rock categories was growing, with certain growing pains perhaps a built-in result. For lovers of surreal juxtapositions, the results could be fascinating. In the Best New Artist category, for instance, Welsh sensation Tom Jones ultimately triumphed over the likes of not just Herman's Hermits but also jazz pianist and composer Horst Jankowski. History does not record whether Herman's Hermits and Jankowski drowned their sorrows together at the bar afterward.

Prior to this "Best on Record" airing, the 8th Annual Grammys were presented at a dinner at the Beverly Hilton Hotel in Beverly Hills—with Jerry Lewis on board to emcee—as well as simultaneous events by Recording Academy chapters in New York, Chicago, and Nashville.

*Left page clockwise from top left: Roger Miller • Bill Cosby • Perry Como • Diahann Carroll This page: Duke Ellington and Tony Bennett*

---

**WINNER SNAPSHOT**
**Record of the Year**
"A Taste of Honey" • Herb Alpert and The Tijuana Brass
**Album of the Year**
*September of My Years* • Frank Sinatra
**Song of the Year**
"The Shadow of Your Smile" (Love theme from The Sandpiper) • Johnny Mandel & Paul Francis Webster, songwriters

**Best New Artist**
Tom Jones

**SPECIAL MERIT AWARDS**
Bing Crosby Award
Duke Ellington

Thanks in large part to the massive crossover success of his song "King of the Road," the gifted and witty singer/songwriter Roger Miller was the king of the night. Following his five wins at the 7th Annual Grammy Awards, Miller won six more Grammys the second time around during the 8th Awards—Best Country & Western Song; Best Country & Western Vocal Performance, Male; Best Country & Western Single; Best Country & Western Album; as well as Best Contemporary (R&R) Vocal Performance, Male; and Best Contemporary (R&R) Single. Indeed, "King of the Road" proved so overwhelmingly popular with voters that "Queen of the House," a soundalike female answer record by Jody Miller (no relation), was itself deemed to be the Best Country & Western Vocal Performance, Female.

The Chairman of the Board was also royalty on this Grammy night. Frank Sinatra's brilliantly brooding song cycle *September of My Years*, produced by Sonny Burke, won Album of the Year, while Sinatra's "It Was a Very Good Year" also took the award for Best Vocal Performance, Male, over Paul McCartney for his performance on the Beatles' "Yesterday."

Another of the big winners at the 8th Annual Grammy Awards—Herb Alpert and The Tijuana Brass—won three awards, including Record of the Year for "A Taste of Honey," and were given the honor of being the first musical performers on "The Best on Record" NBC special. No less than Bob Hope opened the show, coyly referring to generational divisions in show business when he noted that the special featured "just about every great artist in the musical world with the exception of Sonny & Cher. We hoped to have them but Sonny didn't have a tuxedo and Cher wouldn't loan him hers." Hope also offered a little history lesson for the new generation of music lovers, holding up an award and helpfully explaining, "This is a Grammy—that's short for gramophone for those of you who were born post–Frankie Avalon. From this crude hand-cranked instrument has sprung the billion-dollar recording industry."

Whatever divisions were at work within the industry, there were sublime Grammy moments on this "Best on Record" show, none more so than when Grammy winner Duke Ellington teamed up with Tony Bennett to perform "Don't Get Around Much Anymore." On the show, following a tribute from Dinah Shore, Bennett handed Ellington the third ever Bing Crosby Award. In a charming if seemingly scripted moment, Ellington then asked Bennett if he and his group could have "the pleasure of merging our dulcet cacophony with the melodic contour of your aural facet of agreeability." Ellington and Bennett's altogether stunning collaboration was so gorgeous a musical merger that, watching two masters at work, it was hard to think any controversies or generational tensions could matter.

Left page clockwise from top left: *Don Adams • Phyllis Diller and Shelly Manne at the Los Angeles awards dinner • Bob Hope • Mort Sahl, Jerry Lewis, and Louis Armstrong at the Los Angeles awards dinner* This page: *Jerry Moss and Herb Alpert at the Los Angeles awards dinner*

*Did You Know ...?* *The Byrds, Marilyn Maye, Sonny & Cher, and Glenn Yarbrough, along with Herman's Hermits, Horst Jankowski, and Tom Jones, are also nominated for Best New Artist.* • *Frank Sinatra's* September of My Years *also wins in Best Album Notes for Stan Cornyn and his "It Was a Very Good Year" also wins in Best Arrangement Accompanying a Vocalist or Instrumentalist for Gordon Jenkins.* • *James Brown earns his first nomination and win for "Papa's Got a Brand New Bag" in Best Rhythm & Blues Recording.* • *Leopold Stokowski enjoys his only win for* Ives: Symphony No. 4 *in Classical Performance, Orchestra.*

# 9th Annual Grammy Awards

AWARDS DINNERS HELD IN
CHICAGO, LOS ANGELES, NASHVILLE, AND NEW YORK

*Eligibility Year: November 2, 1965–November 1, 1966*
*Announced on March 2, 1967*
"The Best on Record" airs on May 24, 1967

*Held during* a period of tremendous cultural transition for the country and only a matter of months before the Summer of Love, the 9th Annual Grammy Awards reflected a certain amount of love and peace between music's past, present, and future. This was, for instance, a year when The Academy recognized the achievements of both the Chairman of the Board and the Fab Four. Sinatra's recording of "Strangers in the Night" was named Record of the Year and *A Man and His Music* was awarded Album of the Year. Sinatra also received the Best Vocal Performance, Male, award for "Strangers in the Night."

The Song of the Year Grammy, on the other hand, went to John Lennon and Paul McCartney for "Michelle" recorded by the Beatles, and McCartney also won the Best Contemporary (R&R) Solo Vocal Performance, Male or Female, for "Eleanor Rigby"—with that abbreviation of "rock and roll" in parentheses perhaps grammatically reflecting some slight ambivalence about the rock music now impacting the pop categories. The Beatles' groundbreaking *Revolver* was also honored for Best Album Cover, Graphic

Arts, for the work of Klaus Voormann, a friend of the band since their days in Hamburg, Germany.

When "The Best on Record" show aired in May, it too reflected the marked duality of the music that was on the airwaves in 1966. After a show introduction from Steve Lawrence, in which he noted, "If music happens to be your bag, I know we couldn't drive you away from this set with a long-playing used car commercial," Tony Randall introduced the first musical number of the show: a retro yet trippy performance of "Winchester Cathedral" by the New Vaudeville Band, which won the Best Contemporary (R&R) Recording, despite not being terribly R *or* R. During the song, at least one member of the group could be seen sipping tea. Afterward, Peter Noone of Herman's Hermits fame noted, "I must be honest, personally I found them a bit *raucous*—musically."

Restoring some order, Robert Preston, star of Meredith Willson's *The Music Man*, introduced a candle-lit performance by Eydie Gorme, the Grammy winner for Best Vocal Performance, Female ("If He Walked into My Life")—a

Left page: *Ray Charles*
This page: *New Vaudeville Band*

**WINNER SNAPSHOT**
**Record of the Year**
"Strangers in the Night" • Frank Sinatra
**Album of the Year**
*A Man and His Music* • Frank Sinatra
**Song of the Year**
"Michelle" • John Lennon & Paul McCartney, songwriters

**SPECIAL MERIT AWARDS**
Bing Crosby Award
Ella Fitzgerald

Trustees Award
Georg Solti & John Culshaw

51

decision that he declared was "more unanimous than a Russian election." The win for Jerry Herman in the Best Score from an Original Cast Show Album for *Mame* was celebrated with a rousing appearance by Louis Armstrong singing the Broadway smash's title song. Actress Edie Adams saucily referenced Herman's earlier success with *Hello, Dolly!* by noting, "He scored with *Dolly* and he scored with *Mame* and got a Grammy for both—which makes him one of the most celebrated bigamists on Broadway."

After singing a few bars of "I Can't Stop Loving You," Frankie Avalon and Buddy Greco joked that anyone who sings like Ray Charles was "Italian, whether he wants to be or not." They then introduced Charles as "one of the greatest Italian singers," before the Genius of Soul performed his classic version of "Crying Time," for which he had won the Grammys for Best Rhythm & Blues Recording and Best R&B Solo Vocal Performance, Male or Female. The most surreally intriguing introduction on this "Best on Record," however, *had* to be Liberace's comments before a fantastically psychedelic rock video for the Beatles' "Strawberry Fields Forever" was played: "England has produced a variety of talent ranging all the way from Richard Burton to Twiggy. This next group is somewhere in between."

On a show where almost every presenter and performer wore formal evening wear, Liberace continued a running joke about the wild fashions currently enjoyed by the younger generation. The long-haired Beatles, he said, could take some credit for kicking off the Carnaby Street mod clothing fad "that all the kids are wearing today. I guess if you're young and enjoy wearing garish clothing, there's really no harm in it," he said.

Before introducing the Anita Kerr Singers—winners of the Best Performance by a Vocal Group ("A Man and a Woman")—comedian Godfrey Cambridge got off a few topical lines, again taking a swing at the hippies' affinity for long hair: "I guess you've heard that the Mamas and the Papas are expecting a baby. They can hardly wait. It'll be the first time they really know which is the Mamas and which is the Papas." (The California quartet took home the Best Contemporary [R&R] Group Performance, Vocal or Instrumental, Grammy for their radiant hit "Monday, Monday.")

Pat Boone then awarded Ella Fitzgerald the Bing Crosby Award for outstanding artistic contribution, after which she performed "Satin Doll" and "Don't Be That Way," bedecked in a shimmery red gown. She was ably backed by the telecast's music director, Les Brown, who helmed the show's house band.

Finally, Sammy Davis Jr. wrapped up the hour with a true touch of Rat Pack genius as only he could. Dramatically smoking a cigarette, Davis explained, "A phonograph record can be a magical thing. It can make you laugh, make you cry, lift you up, let you down easy. It can make you wig out, and even more important—if you've got the right kind of sounds, man—it can make *her* wig out over you."

Left page clockwise from top: *John Phillips, Michelle Phillips, Denny Doherty, and Herb Alpert at the Los Angeles awards dinner • Davy Jones signs autographs at the Los Angeles awards dinner • Wes Montgomery* This page: *Steve Lawrence, Eydie Gorme, and Tony Bennett*

*Did You Know ...?* Neal Hefti's "Batman Theme" wins the Grammy for Best Instrumental Theme. Hefti's album for "The Odd Couple" would receive two nominations at the 11th Grammys. • The Beach Boys, Loretta Lynn, the Mamas and the Papas, Lou Rawls, and Stevie Wonder all receive their first nominations. • Edward R. Murrow wins for Edward R. Murrow: A Reporter Remembers—Vol. 1 The War Years in Best Spoken Word, Documentary or Drama Recording.

# 10th Annual Grammy Awards

The 10th Annual Grammy Awards were notable on many levels, and not simply because this award year marked the first decade of Grammy history. This was also, for instance, a wide-ranging year of winners in which the formerly scandalous rocker Elvis Presley won Best Sacred Performance for his *How Great Thou Art* album, Republican Illinois Senator Everett M. Dirksen won Best Spoken Word, Documentary or Drama Recording (*Gallant Men*), while veteran horror movie great Boris Karloff received the Grammy for Best Recording for Children for what has become the holiday perennial *Dr. Seuss: How the Grinch Stole Christmas.*

With comedian Stan Freberg emceeing the Los Angeles dinner awards announcement that preceded "The Best on Record" show, the 10th Grammy Awards would also prove a suitably high-flying year for the vocal group the 5th Dimension, who achieved impressive upward mobility by taking home no less than four Grammys for their rendition of Jimmy Webb's "Up, Up and Away"—Record of the Year, Best Performance by a Vocal Group, Best Contemporary Single, and Best Contemporary Group Performance (Vocal or Instrumental)—while Webb's song itself was named Song of the Year. As if that wasn't enough for Webb, the Johnny Mann Singers' rendition of "Up, Up and Away" also took the Grammy for Best Performance by a Chorus.

This year would also prove the scant degrees of separation and the broad connections between musical genres.

Webb was also responsible for "By the Time I Get to Phoenix," for which Glen Campbell won Best Vocal Performance, Male, and Best Contemporary Male Solo Vocal Performance. And Campbell's winning ways didn't end there, as his version of John Hartford's "Gentle on My Mind" was named Best Country & Western Recording and Best Country & Western Solo Vocal Performance, Male. Spreading the "Gentle" love further, the Grammys for Best Folk Performance and Best Country & Western Song were bestowed on Hartford himself.

**WINNER SNAPSHOT**
**Record of the Year**
"Up, Up and Away" • The 5th Dimension
**Album of the Year**
*Sgt. Pepper's Lonely Hearts Club Band* • The Beatles
**Song of the Year**
"Up, Up and Away" • Jimmy L. Webb, songwriter
**Best New Artist**
Bobbie Gentry

**SPECIAL MERIT AWARDS**
Bing Crosby Award
Irving Berlin

Trustees Award
Duke Ellington & Billy Strayhorn,
Krzysztof Penderecki

Future Glen Campbell duet partner Bobbie Gentry also enjoyed an exceedingly warm welcome to the Grammys, winning Best Vocal Performance, Female, and Best Contemporary Female Solo Vocal Performance for her startling and cryptic story song "Ode to Billie Joe," as well as the Grammy for Best New Artist. The awards presentations were made at dinners in four cities this year: Chicago, Los Angeles, Nashville, and New York, with performers ranging from Woody Herman and Ramsey Lewis to Joe Tex and the Mothers of Invention.

Some group by the name of the Beatles, meanwhile, did fairly fabulously themselves— winning the Grammys for Album of the Year and Best Contemporary Album for *Sgt. Pepper's Lonely Hearts Club Band*—a certified Summer of Love classic that was also recognized with the awards for Best Engineered Recording, Non-Classical, for Geoff Emerick and Best Album Cover, Graphic Arts, for art directors Peter Blake and Jann Haworth.

The Grammys' 10th anniversary was duly noted on NBC's Timex-sponsored "The Best on Record: The Grammy Awards Show" (as it was now officially known) when Glen Campbell, Bobbie Gentry, Chet Atkins, and Jack Jones performed a medley of past Song of the Year winners. This was one highlight in a show in which the outstanding performances ranged from an astounding, soulful rendition of "Dead End Street" by Lou Rawls,

winner of the Best R&B Solo Vocal Performance, Male, Grammy, and a filmed appearance (taken from a United Nations human rights benefit concert) featuring Yehudi Menuhin and Ravi Shankar's *West Meets East*, which won for Best Chamber Music Performance.

The show continued to reveal the Grammys' willingness to take some chances, featuring soon-to-become Grammy semi-regular Tommy Smothers, then under fire for comments about the Vietnam War and other topics on his own show. In introducing Glen Campbell, Smothers suggested Campbell had won "Best Male Performance," a comment he finished with a wink and a nod.

This was also the year on "The Best on Record" show when the always-helpful Andy Williams (future host of the first live Grammy telecast) tried to sum up what the Grammy meant to artists. "These are the Grammys," Williams explained. "Herb Alpert uses them for earrings. Henry Mancini uses them for doorstops. The Beatles paid off their guru with four or five." Then referencing his own failure to win a Grammy, Williams noted, "LBJ is proudest of me—I haven't taken *any* gold out of circulation." Yet Williams made a more serious point when he went on to say of the Grammy, "This is the Oscar, the Emmy, the Tony of the recording industry." Indeed, that was exactly the luster the Grammy had now taken on.

Left page clockwise from top left: *Lou Rawls • Davy Jones and Angie Dickinson at the Los Angeles awards dinner • TV promo featuring Bobbie Gentry • Benny Goodman and Morton Gould at the New York awards dinner • Cass Elliot and Tommy Smothers at the Los Angeles awards dinner*
This page: *Duke Ellington*

*Did You Know ...?* Legend Aretha Franklin receives her first nominations and wins. She wins for "Respect" in Best Rhythm & Blues Recording and in Best Rhythm & Blues Solo Vocal Performance, Female. Franklin goes on to earn 42 nominations with 17 wins over a period of 38 years, with her most current win in 2005. • Pierre Boulez gets his first wins. They are as the conductor for Berg: Wozzeck in Album of the Year, Classical, and in Best Opera Recording. Boulez will go on to receive 65 nominations with 26 wins. • Composer Burt Bacharach gets his first win, for "Alfie" in Best Instrumental Arrangement. • Frank Sinatra and daughter Nancy Sinatra are nominated in Record of the Year for "Somethin' Stupid."

THE BEST ON RECORD

THE GRAMMY AWARDS SHOW

# 11th Annual Grammy Awards

AWARDS DINNERS HELD IN
CHICAGO, LOS ANGELES, NASHVILLE, AND NEW YORK

*Eligibility Year: November 2, 1967–November 1, 1968*
*Announced on March 12, 1969*
*"The Best on Record" airs on May 5, 1969*

For the 11th Annual Grammy Awards, the live presentation ceremony and "The Best on Record" special were linked as never before—bringing the show one step closer to the live telecast that would follow in two years. The winner for Record of the Year was not announced during the awards dinner so that the winner could instead be revealed during the NBC special that aired nearly two months later on May 5. To accomplish this, five separate awards announcements and acceptance speeches were taped. Just an hour before air time, a network official opened the envelope and instructed a machine operator to insert the correct reel into the master tape. The decision proved somewhat controversial. Writing in the *Los Angeles Times*, staff writer Wayne Warga reported that when Los Angeles Chapter President Irving Townsend announced at the awards dinner that an award was being held back to help ratings, "The audience booed him. Fortunately, nobody threw anything. This was probably because the waiters had wisely cleared the tables." Apparently performances by Jackie DeShannon, Lou Rawls, Tommy Boyce & Bobby Hart, and Bill Medley were far better received.

There was no booing whatsoever when "The Best on Record" finally aired—indeed, this edition of "The Best on Record: The Grammy Awards Show" felt downright giddy, thanks in part to the presence of opening and closing act Dan Rowan and Dick Martin, whose *Laugh-In* show had become the comedic rage since its debut in 1968. Interestingly, *Rowan & Martin's Laugh-In* was—like "The Best on Record"—produced by George Schlatter, a synergy that lent the proceeding a certain *Laugh-In* like, slightly off-color, "sock-it-to-me" charm.

Accordingly, comedians figured quite prominently in this hour of TV. Flip Wilson introduced Jeannie C. Riley's performance of "Harper Valley P.T.A."—a winner for Best Country Vocal Performance,

*Left page: Promotional illustration depicting, clockwise from top, Jose Feliciano, Dionne Warwick, Glen Campbell, the cast of* Hair, *and Jeannie C. Riley*
**This page:** *Jackie DeShannon and Micky Dolenz at the Los Angeles awards dinner*

**WINNER SNAPSHOT**
**Record of the Year**
"Mrs. Robinson" • Simon & Garfunkel
**Album of the Year**
*By the Time I Get to Phoenix* • Glen Campbell
**Song of the Year**
"Little Green Apples" • Bobby Russell, songwriter
**Best New Artist**
Jose Feliciano

Female, and a nominee in the still open Record of the Year category—by declaring, "Country music has come a long way since the washboard and kazoo. Nowadays they use electric washboards and electric kazoos." Don Rickles appeared alongside Tiny Tim for a surreal introduction of a fascinating and unusual clip of another of the Record of the Year nominees—Simon & Garfunkel's "Mrs. Robinson." Asked to film a performance of the song, Simon & Garfunkel suggested instead that they would prefer to film a segment at an empty Yankee Stadium— a seeming nod to Joe DiMaggio who figured in the song's lyrics. Executive Producer Ted Bergmann recalls Paul Simon saying, "Art and I will run the bases while you play 'Mrs. Robinson.'" The resulting clip is a fantastic, offbeat early rock video—a truly winning non-performance Grammy performance. Tommy Smothers introduced the Los Angeles cast of *Hair*, which then performed two songs from *The American Tribal Love Rock Musical*, spotlighting both Delores Hall and Jennifer Warnes, the latter of whom would return to win a couple Grammys more than a decade later.

It took a village—okay, actually the entire King Family—to introduce Best New Artist and Best

Contemporary Pop Vocal Performance, Male, winner Jose Feliciano, and the singer/guitarist did the whole family proud with a powerful rendition of "Light My Fire." Burt Bacharach introduced a strong performance of "Do You Know the Way to San Jose?" by Dionne Warwick—Grammy winner for Best Contemporary Pop Vocal Performance, Female. "She has a voice and a style and a warmth that gives any song a very special meaning," he said, clearly from personal experience. Mama Cass, meanwhile, introduced a performance clip of "Hey Jude" by the Beatles— another nominee for Record of the Year.

Toward the end of "The Best on Record," Henry Mancini appeared to introduce "the big one we've all waited for"—the winner of Record of the Year. Ultimately Simon & Garfunkel's "Mrs. Robinson" prevailed over not only the Beatles' "Hey Jude," but also Jeannie C. Riley's "Harper Valley P.T.A.," Glen Campbell's "Wichita Lineman," and Bobby Goldsboro's "Honey." Accordingly, the pretaped speech came from Art Garfunkel who, wearing a tux but holding a baseball, graciously—and theoretically—accepted on behalf of producer and engineer Roy Halee and "my best friend Paul Simon who wouldn't wear a tuxedo today."

*Did You Know ...?* Supergroup Cream is nominated for Best New Artist. • Otis Redding wins Best R&B Vocal Performance, Male, for "(Sittin' on) The Dock of the Bay" posthumously. • Jeannie C. Riley is the first country artist to be nominated for Best New Artist.

# 1970s

Tom Wolfe dubbed the '70s the "Me Decade,"

but this troubled and sometimes excessive age of Watergate and Jimmy Carter,

sensitive singer/songwriters and hardcore funk, the death of Elvis and the birth of punk,

also brought the world the Grammy Awards as we now know them—a live event

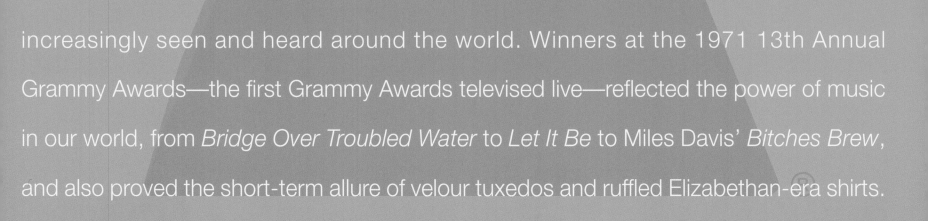

increasingly seen and heard around the world. Winners at the 1971 13th Annual Grammy Awards—the first Grammy Awards televised live—reflected the power of music in our world, from *Bridge Over Troubled Water* to *Let It Be* to Miles Davis' *Bitches Brew*, and also proved the short-term allure of velour tuxedos and ruffled Elizabethan-era shirts.

# 12th Annual Grammy Awards

## AWARDS DINNERS HELD IN
### ATLANTA, CHICAGO, LOS ANGELES, NASHVILLE, AND NEW YORK

*Eligibility Year: November 2, 1968–November 1, 1969*
*Announced on March 11, 1970*
"The Best on Record" airs on May 7, 1970

The 12th Annual Grammy Awards should go down in history for at least two major reasons. First, this would be the very last "Best on Record" show before the Grammys once and for all transformed into an annual live telecast event. Second, this was also the year that comedy great Bob Newhart actually chose to wear a green tuxedo on the show, a fashion choice that will live in a sort of charming *Austin Powers*-ish infamy.

Presented on NBC, and thankfully in "living color," this "Best on Record" show was more than simply a fascinating time capsule of '70s fashion. This year's studio-based Grammy telecast suggested that the time had come to take the great leap forward to a live telecast, both because the actual presentations had now grown to an unwieldy five simultaneous dinners across the country, and since this final taped show revealed "The Best on Record" had become a curious hybrid of *Rowan & Martin's Laugh-In* and a pre-MTV video clip program. The show opened with smooth crooner Jack Jones in a sort of brown vest-dress singing the soon-to-be much

recorded "Games People Play," which won both Song of the Year and Best Contemporary Song for the song's writer, Joe South, who also had the first hit version. Further evidence of the song's popularity was that soul sax great King Curtis also won Best R&B Instrumental Performance for *his* version of "Games People Play."

As was now tradition, the actual Grammy presentation dinners were star-studded and far-flung. Bill Cosby—who once again won the award for Best Comedy Recording—was the master of ceremonies in Los Angeles, while those duties were handled by Merv Griffin in New York, Regis Philbin in Chicago, Jack Palance in Nashville, and Ray Stevens and Steve Alaimo in Atlanta.

Among the other big winners during the first Grammy presentation to be held in the '70s was the jazz-rock horn band Blood, Sweat & Tears, who won Grammys for Album of the Year (*Blood, Sweat & Tears*) and Best Contemporary Instrumental Performance ("Variations on a Theme by Eric Satie"), while Fred

**Left page:**
*Dionne Warwick*
**This page:** *Pat Paulsen, Burt Bacharach, and Tina Turner at the Los Angeles awards dinner*

**WINNER SNAPSHOT**
**Record of the Year**
"Aquarius/Let the Sunshine In (the Flesh Failures)" • The 5th Dimension
**Album of the Year**
*Blood, Sweat & Tears* • Blood, Sweat & Tears
**Song of the Year**
"Games People Play" • Joe South, songwriter
**Best New Artist**
Crosby, Stills & Nash

**SPECIAL MERIT AWARDS**
Trustees Award
Robert Moog

Lipsius won Best Arrangement Accompanying Vocalist(s) for the group's smash "Spinning Wheel." The gig of introducing Blood, Sweat & Tears on "The Best on Record" show fell to Sammy Davis Jr. who did not disappoint, providing some of his fantastically charming patter. "BS&T have accomplished the impossible," Davis noted of the group who had an impressive four nominations for the year. "They have spanned the generation gap, the communication gap, the credibility gap, the sex gap, and, yeah baby, the color gap. Everybody digs them." Instead of a live performance, the show then featured a sort of early rock video of the band hanging on the road as "Spinning Wheel" played.

Yet the most unforgettable and downright surreal video of the show had to be Peggy Lee's "Is That All There Is?," the year's winner for Best Contemporary Vocal Performance, Female, and a nominee for Record of the Year—a category once again revealed live at the end of "The Best on Record" telecast. Lee appeared alone in the Waldorf Astoria ballroom—emphatically *not* singing the verses of the song. The result was strangely brilliant, as if David Lynch were suddenly directing the Grammy show.

Meanwhile, the single most soulful performance—and possibly the most fiercely funky ever—belonged to the Isley Brothers. Introduced by Sonny & Cher—who showed the humorous flair that would launch their comedy hour the next year—as "the only act that can drown us out," the Isleys proceeded to whip up a fantastic and slightly frenzied rendition of "It's Your Thing," which won the Grammy for Best R&B Vocal Performance by a Duo or Group.

Other notable winners included Joni Mitchell's Grammy for Best Folk Performance for *Clouds*, Quincy Jones' victory for Best Instrumental Jazz Performance, Large Group or Soloist with Large Group, for *Walking in Space*, and Harry Nilsson's win for Best Contemporary Vocal Performance, Male, for his version of "Everybody's Talkin'" from the soundtrack to the film *Midnight Cowboy*.

In the country music world, two future icons won, with Tammy Wynette taking home the Grammy for Best Country Vocal Performance, Female, for her classic "Stand by Your Man," while Johnny Cash won Best Country Vocal Performance, Male, for "A Boy Named Sue." Interestingly, the Man in Black wasn't just honored for his vocal performance, but his literary performance as well, as he received the Best Album Notes award for his contributions to his friend Bob Dylan's *Nashville Skyline*.

"A Boy Named Sue"—written by cartoonist and children's book author Shel Silverstein—was also honored as Best Country Song, a moment in history noted by Bob Newhart who, in introducing Cash, confessed, "I'm a little worried what historians are going to think of us when they discover one of the biggest songs of my era was entitled 'A Boy Named Sue.'" Ultimately, Newhart probably should have been a little less worried about that song and a little more concerned about that green tux.

Left page clockwise from top left:
*The 5th Dimension • The Isley Brothers • Sonny & Cher • Harry Nilsson, Joni Mitchell, and Gary Owens at the Los Angeles awards dinner*
This page: *Johnny Cash*

*Did You Know ...?* Led Zeppelin is nominated for Best New Artist, their only nomination during their years as a band. • Walter Carlos (later Wendy Carlos after a sex change) earns three wins the first time nominated. He wins Album of the Year, Classical, and Best Classical Instrumental Performance—Instrumental Soloist or Soloists (with or without Orchestra) for Switched-On Bach and as the engineer for Switched-On Bach in Best Engineered Recording, Classical. • Bob Dylan receives his first country nomination, for "Nashville Skyline Rag" in Best Country Instrumental Performance. • B.B. King gets his first of 29 nominations (with 14 wins to date), for the album Live and Well in Best R&B Vocal Performance, Male.

# 13th Annual Grammy Awards

HOLLYWOOD PALLADIUM, HOLLYWOOD

*Eligibility Year: November 2, 1969–October 15, 1970*
*Announced on March 16, 1971*

*For the* Grammy Awards, 13 would prove to be an extremely lucky number. For the first time in its history, the show had its very first live telecast—a significant departure from the previous pretaped broadcasts showcasing certain winners a month or two after the Awards presentation. Finally, the excitement of the Grammys could be enjoyed by viewers in real time.

And there was a lot to enjoy. Imagine Andy Williams delivering a joke about John Lennon appearing nude on the cover of the *Two Virgins* album (actual punch line: "The cover proved that John isn't one of the Lennon Sisters") or a cultural event in which jazz legend Duke Ellington and *The Partridge Family* hunk David Cassidy appear back-to-back in the list of stars, and you've imagined the kind of broad cultural landscape the Grammy Awards often traverse on a single show. You've also pretty clearly imagined the 13th annual telecast rightly billed as being "for the first time live from Hollywood."

In great Grammy tradition, the show offered many fascinating examples of the counterculture and the old

guard mixing and mingling in surprising and entertaining ways. It was telling that one of Williams' most successful opening gags involved trying to find a group that would appeal to everyone—to which he, of course, suggested the Grand Funk Tabernacle Choir. This would also prove to be a big Grammy night for both Paul Simon and Art Garfunkel and Karen and Richard Carpenter, all of whom took home multiple major awards.

This 90-minute show was centered around performances of the five songs nominated for Song of the Year, often shot through beads, abstract stage designs, and other '70s style artifacts. Ray Stevens' "Everything Is Beautiful" was sung by the Osmond Brothers, who were dressed a bit like Elvis for the occasion. The Carpenters played their own "We've Only Just Begun." Anne Murray sang James Taylor's "Fire and Rain," with dancers dressed like flames heating things up around her. Aretha Franklin sang "Bridge Over Troubled Water" as Simon and Garfunkel watched from the audience. And finally, Dionne Warwick offered up an elegant take on the Beatles' "Let It Be." The winner was

**Left page:** *Linda and Paul McCartney*
**This page:** *Phil Spector presents at the post-telecast ceremony*

---

**WINNER SNAPSHOT**
**Record of the Year**
"Bridge Over Troubled Water" • Simon & Garfunkel
**Album of the Year**
*Bridge Over Troubled Water* • Simon & Garfunkel
**Song of the Year**
"Bridge Over Troubled Water" • Paul Simon, songwriter
**Best New Artist**
Carpenters

**SPECIAL MERIT AWARDS**
Bing Crosby Award
Elvis Presley

Trustees Award
Chris Albertson, John Hammond,
Larry Hiller, Paul Weston

Paul Simon for writing "Bridge Over Troubled Water"—an award presented by master songwriter Burt Bacharach, who would repeat that role several times through the years, most recently at the 49th awards in the company of Seal. Simon, who would later serve as a Grammy host, was especially terse in giving his thanks this night: just a nod. *Bridge Over Troubled Water* also won Album of the Year, while the title track took Record of the Year, Best Contemporary Song, and Best Arrangement Accompanying Vocalists. While accepting the awards, the tension between the duo, who had recently called it quits, was palpable at the podium, and they departed in opposite directions.

The Carpenters, meanwhile, won both Best New Artist (over Elton John *and* the Partridge Family) and Best Contemporary Vocal Performance by a Duo, Group or Chorus for "Close to You."

The nominees for Best Country Song were also performed by an impressive array of singers—Charley Pride, Conway Twitty, Wanda Jackson, Marty Robbins, and a nearly clean-cut Hank Williams Jr. who did Merle Haggard's "Fightin' Side of Me." The winner, "My Woman, My Woman, My Wife," was written and performed by Marty Robbins.

The political climate also made its mark: The late Martin Luther King Jr.'s *Why I Oppose the Vietnam War* took home the Grammy for Best Spoken Word Recording.

Yet possibly the most memorable presentation of the night—besides an entertainingly sloppy and much referenced presentation by soul singer/songwriter Brook Benton who seemed to be speaking more gibberish than English, and after which Williams jokingly reminded the audience, "We're coming to you live tonight …"—came when another Duke besides Ellington took the stage to present a Grammy—John Wayne himself, who presented the award for Best Original Score Written for a Motion Picture or Television Special. The Grammy went to the Beatles for the Phil Spector-produced *Let It Be* (an album and quasi-documentary film) over such other distinguished nominees as Johnny Mercer with Henry Mancini (*Darling Lili*), Alfred Newman (*Airport*), Johnny Mandel (*M*A*S*H*), and Fred Karlin (*The Sterile Cuckoo*). Paul McCartney clearly thrilled the crowd by appearing to accept the award, bringing his wife Linda onstage. The surprise last-minute appearance was a well-guarded secret with only a few Grammy officials aware that the first live telecast would be graced by an appearance by the man they call the Cute One.

Though McCartney's actual acceptance comments were exceedingly brief ("Thank you. Goodnight."), the visual of the happy couple standing beside the great Western star remains forever priceless—True Grit with a real Beatle.

Left page clockwise from top: *The Osmonds • Art Garfunkel and Paul Simon • Charley Pride* This page: *Richard and Karen Carpenter*

*Did You Know …?* Michael Jackson earns his first Grammy nomination as part of the Jackson 5 for "ABC." • Miles Davis' Bitches Brew *wins in a jazz category, his first Grammy in 10 years since* Sketches of Spain *won.*

# 14th Annual Grammy Awards

*Eligibility Year: October 16, 1970–October 15, 1971*
*Announced on March 14, 1972*

The '70s would prove, among many other things, to be the era of the sensitive singer/songwriter, and being a great one would prove a rewarding experience at the 14th Annual Grammy Awards held at New York's Felt Forum (now The Theater at Madison Square Garden). Broadcast live on ABC for the second year and hosted again by Andy Williams, the Grammy Awards were dominated by a woman who was on the opposite coast with a newborn child—Carole King, who won Record of the Year ("It's Too Late"), Album of the Year (*Tapestry*), Song of the Year ("You've Got a Friend"), and Best Pop Vocal Performance, Female (*Tapestry*). And as if that wasn't impressive enough, King's "You've Got a Friend" also helped her friend James Taylor win Best Pop Vocal Performance, Male, while Quincy Jones won Best Pop Instrumental Performance for *Smackwater Jack*, named after another great song King cowrote with early Brill

Building partner and former husband Gerry Goffin.

Andy Williams started the show off by mentioning some records that were *not* nominated, including "Joy to the World" by Archie Bunker of *All in the Family* fame (the groundbreaking sitcom about a lovable bigot had launched in 1971), "I Am ... I Said" by Richard Nixon (his imperious nature would soon lead to Watergate), and "Shaft" as recorded by the James Frey of his day, Clifford Irving (Irving had published a faux "authorized" biography of recluse Howard Hughes).

Then in a nod to the show being held in such close proximity to the Great White Way, Williams introduced the cast of *Godspell* to perform an uplifting medley of two songs from the show: "Prepare Ye the Way of the Lord" and "Day by Day." In a noteworthy time capsule moment, Anthony Newley and the most musical Brady of all, Florence Henderson, presented the award for Best Score from

**WINNER SNAPSHOT**
**Record of the Year**
"It's Too Late" • Carole King
**Album of the Year**
*Tapestry* • Carole King
**Song of the Year**
"You've Got a Friend" • Carole King, songwriter
**Best New Artist**
Carly Simon

**SPECIAL MERIT AWARDS**
Bing Crosby Award
Louis Armstrong,
Mahalia Jackson

Trustees Award
The Beatles

an Original Cast Show Album, which *Godspell* composer Stephen Schwartz accepted in what looked very much like a denim tux.

The now late great Janis Joplin was rightly nominated for Best R&B Vocal Performance, Female, alongside Aretha Franklin, Diana Ross, Freda Payne, and Jean Knight, with the Queen of Soul winning out for her stirring rendition of "Bridge Over Troubled Water." The 5th Dimension did one of their entertaining singing presentations of the nominees, ultimately handing out the Best Pop Vocal Performance by a Duo or Group award to the Carpenters for their self-titled 1971 album, which, in a Beatlesesque nod, became known to fans as "the tan album."

More surprising was the usually stone-faced TV legend Ed Sullivan appearing to present the Grammy for Best Comedy Recording and getting a few laughs at his own expense. "I think it's safe to say that after 23 years on television my comedy talent wasn't obvious to anyone," Sullivan joked. A shot of nominees Cheech & Chong in the audience in full freak regalia makes one wish they had won so that there could be a shot of them and Sullivan embracing, but the award went instead to the great Lily Tomlin

(*This Is a Recording*) who, like several among the night's winners, was not present to accept. Leonard Bernstein was there to pick up a special award, but explained he had a reason to leave early. "I could go on also interminably except that I have to rush back to my television set to see *West Side Story* on the other channel," Bernstein explained. "Don't you turn that dial," host Williams then warned with a smile after Bernstein had exited.

The night offered other pleasant surprises, including a characteristically fine performance by the Bill Evans Trio. Evans didn't smile as he played, but broke into a grin after winning the Grammy for Best Jazz Performance by a Group for *The Bill Evans Album*—one of his two awards for the night. Williams offered a preview of the upcoming film of *The Concert for Bangladesh* and later presented a Trustees Award to an absent Beatles, explaining, "They were a revelation and a revolution."

But sometimes such absences were charming. When King won her third award for the night for Record of the Year, Herb Alpert—presenting with Karen and Richard Carpenter—smiled and said, "*Well*, she had triplets."

Left page clockwise from top: *Three Dog Night • Aretha Franklin • Conway Twitty and Loretta Lynn* This page: *Richard Harris and Isaac Hayes*

# 15th Annual Grammy Awards

*L*ike *several* other Grammy shows of the era, the 15th Annual Grammy Awards ceremony—broadcast live from Nashville's Tennessee Theatre and hosted by Andy Williams—seems in retrospect to be an intermittently mind-blowing, impressively eclectic study in contrasts, from a first performance by the decidedly clean-cut Mike Curb Congregation to the Album of the Year award going to *The Concert for Bangladesh*, the spiritual predecessor of such global pop goodwill efforts as USA for Africa, Live 8, and Live Aid.

Taking his cue from the previous year's name-game jokes, host Andy Williams kidded about some songs that weren't nominated—including "Last Tango in Paris" by Henry Kissinger, "One Less Bell to Answer" by heavyweight fighter Joe Frazier, "I Am Woman" by Alice Cooper (jokes about Cooper's gender-bending name would become a running gag for the next few years), and Burt Reynolds' version of "Superfly."

Williams then introduced a convincing performance of "Your Mama Don't Dance" by Loggins & Messina, nominees for Best New Artist. Immediately afterward, the 5th Dimension offered a singing presentation of the nominees and the award went to America on the strength of the megahit "A Horse with No Name," with Dusty Springfield accepting on their behalf.

This night in Nashville then took a country turn with Charley Pride performing "Kiss an Angel Good Mornin'," followed by Loretta Lynn and Eddy Arnold presenting him with the Grammy for Best Country Vocal Performance, Male (it also nabbed Best Country Song for songwriter Ben Peters). The Staple Singers then gave one of the most inspiring and inspired performances of the night with their Stax soul gospel masterpiece, "I'll Take You There," with Mavis Staples in particularly fine form.

In arguably the night's most unlikely pairing, the

**WINNER SNAPSHOT**
**Record of the Year**
"The First Time Ever I Saw Your Face" • Roberta Flack
**Album of the Year**
*The Concert for Bangladesh* • George Harrison, Ravi Shankar, Bob Dylan, Leon Russell, Ringo Starr, Billy Preston, Eric Clapton & Klaus Voormann
**Song of the Year**
"The First Time Ever I Saw Your Face" • Ewan MacColl, songwriter

**Best New Artist**
America

wonderfully tough-talking comedienne Moms Mabley was partnered with wholesome singer Johnny Mann of the Johnny Mann Singers to present the next award for Best R&B Vocal Performance by a Duo, Group or Chorus. Donning her glasses and looking Mann over, Mabley told the crowd with perfect timing, "You all *got* to be kidding." The award went to the Temptations for "Papa Was a Rollin' Stone," with their old friend Smokey Robinson accepting (the song would win three Grammys on the night for the group, arranger Paul Riser, and songwriters Barrett Strong and Norman Whitfield).

The show's mind-bending eclecticism continued for the rest of the night, from Donna Fargo singing the impossibly upbeat "Happiest Girl in the Whole USA" (and winning Best Country Vocal Performance, Female) to Curtis Mayfield and some funky interracial dancers in glitter Afros performing the gritty junkie lament "Freddie's Dead" from *Superfly*. In between were some of the year's biggest hits, including Mac Davis' "Baby Don't Get Hooked on Me" and Gilbert O'Sullivan's "Alone Again (Naturally)."

Other highlights of this Grammy evening included the great Johnny Cash delivering a little Recording Academy history like it was a great American train song. He described the organization as "fast-moving, creative, and exciting like the recording industry itself. I'm Johnny Cash and I'm proud to be a part of it," the Man in Black said in conclusion, as only he could. Close friends Harry Nilsson (who won Best Pop Vocal Performance, Male, for his version of Badfinger's "Without You") and Ringo Starr (who accepted the Album of the Year award on behalf of George Harrison and the other *Concert for Bangladesh* participants) made a memorable award presentation that saw them reading their lines in nearly perfect unison.

And in a wonderful, early display of feminism on the Grammys, Helen Reddy sang her anthem "I Am Woman." Then, in accepting the award for Best Pop Performance, Female, she finished with one of the greatest acceptance lines of all, "... And I would like to thank God because *She* makes everything possible."

Left page clockwise from top:
*Loggins & Messina • Johnny Cash • Michel Legrand and Billy Preston*
This page: *Harry Nilsson and Ringo Starr*

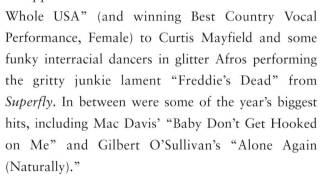

*Did You Know ...?* George Carlin wins his first of four Grammy Awards for the album FM & AM. • *Harry Chapin, the Eagles, Loggins & Messina, and John Prine are all Best New Artist nominees this year.* • The Electric Company *wins Best Recording for Children.*

# 16th Annual Grammy Awards

*Eligibility Year: October 16, 1972–October 15, 1973*
*Announced on March 2, 1974*

Such was the politically charged climate of the times that even consistently amiable host Andy Williams—decked out in a maroon velour tux with wide contrasting black lapels—couldn't help but make a few Watergate references during the 16th Annual Grammy Awards show. Joking about some songs that were *not* nominated during his opening monologue, Williams mentioned "Why Me," as sung by John Ehrlichman, Bob Haldeman, John Mitchell, and "the whole gang" as Williams called the other Watergate coconspirators. Even more cutting was a line that Williams later threw into his introduction of soul great and future Chef on "South Park" Isaac Hayes, whose tremendous musical talents he said, "gave us 'Shaft,' which is what we've been getting for the last couple years."

The 16th Grammy Awards were a loose and lively affair with a number of extremely soulful performances and a series of wonderful, unlikely copresenters. The Jackson 5 teamed with jazz drum legend Shelly Manne to very musically present the first award of the broadcast for Best R&B Vocal Performance by a Duo, Group or Chorus.

The award went to Gladys Knight & the Pips for "Midnight Train to Georgia," the group's first win despite four previous nominations. Knight and the Pips also performed an excellent version of the now classic.

Now in its teen years, these Grammys were a little bawdier than normal as well—hilariously so in the case of Moms Mabley and Kris Kristofferson's unlikely moment as a comedy duo of sorts attempting to present the award for Best Pop Vocal Performance by a Duo, Group or Chorus, also to Gladys Knight & the Pips. Equally entertaining was the extended patter between Helen Reddy and Alice Cooper that found them discussing such pressing issues as the length of his "snake." After being presented with the Grammy for Best Country Vocal Performance, Male, by the unusual partnership of Loretta Lynn and the DeFranco Family, Charlie Rich delivered a smoldering version of "Behind Closed Doors," his unusually carnal country crossover smash. And a pre–Reverend Al Green steamed up the Palladium with "Call Me (Come Back Home)," one of his sultry bedroom smashes.

Left page from top:
*Gladys Knight & the Pips*
*• Karen Carpenter,*
*Bette Midler, and Richard*
*Carpenter*
This page: *Moms Mabley*
*and Kris Kristofferson*

**WINNER SNAPSHOT**
**Record of the Year**
"Killing Me Softly with His Song" • Roberta Flack
**Album of the Year**
*Innervisions* • Stevie Wonder
**Song of the Year**
"Killing Me Softly with His Song" • Charles Fox & Norman Gimbel, songwriters

**Best New Artist**
Bette Midler

The Divine Miss M, Bette Midler, on her way to becoming a huge star with her racy and flamboyant stage act, accepted the Best New Artist award from Karen and Richard Carpenter, whose clean-cut image she had earlier parodied in her shows. "My dear, isn't that a hoot?" Midler said after taking the award from Karen. "I'm surprised she didn't hit me over the head with it."

But at sweet 16, The Academy also showed it was beginning to understand its role in preserving music's legacy. Williams announced the launch of the Grammy Hall of Fame, currently more than 700 titles strong, with the first five inductees: "Body and Soul" by Coleman Hawkins, "The Christmas Song" by Nat "King" Cole, Paul Whiteman's version of Gershwin's "Rhapsody in Blue," "West End Blues" by Louis Armstrong & His Hot Five, and Bing Crosby's "White Christmas" (performed with the Ken Darby Singers).

"Dueling Banjos"—a surprise crossover hit thanks to its appearance in the film *Deliverance*—won Best Country Instrumental Performance for Steve Mandell and Eric Weissberg, the former wearing quite possibly the biggest sideburns in Grammy history. These were also stoned times, and when the smoke cleared the Best Comedy Recording Grammy went to Cheech & Chong for *Los Cochinos*. For reasons related or not, it was also a year marked by a few major sound problems—most notably during Chuck Berry and Little Richard's performing presentation of the award for Best R&B Vocal Performance, Male, to Stevie Wonder for "Superstition"

that found the two rock legends trying to name the nominees during rousing renditions of their greatest hits. They ultimately ended up sharing the one functioning mic, which Berry accused Richard, perhaps characteristically, of trying to keep to himself.

This was also a banner year for two of the most gifted talents of this or any other era—Roberta Flack and Stevie Wonder. Flack and producer Joel Dorn won the Grammy award for Record of the Year for the second year running—this time for "Killing Me Softly with His Song," which also won Song of the Year—an award that went to "The First Time Ever I Saw Your Face" the previous year. Flack also took home the Grammy for Best Pop Vocal Performance, Female.

Wonder—in addition to performing an utterly radiant version of "You Are the Sunshine of My Life"—won five awards this night including Album of the Year for arguably his greatest album ever, *Innervisions*. It was a remarkable triumph for a man who had been comatose for a week in the summer of 1973 after a serious car accident. So it was especially moving when Wonder brought his family onstage with him during his multiple acceptance speeches. Wonder dedicated his Grammy for Best Pop Performance, Male, for "You Are the Sunshine of My Life" to fellow nominee Jim Croce, who had died tragically in a plane crash in September of 1973. He also pointed out his brother Calvin, who had saved his life after the accident, and even allowed his mother to say a few words and express her own appreciation for the "sunshine of *my* life."

**Left page clockwise from top left:** *Helen Reddy and Alice Cooper • Cher • The Jackson 5 and Shelly Manne*
**This page:** *Stevie Wonder*

*Did You Know ...?* Neil Diamond wins his first, and only, Grammy. It is as composer of Jonathan Livingston Seagull *in Album of Best Original Score Written for a Motion Picture or a Television Special. He will have a total of 12 nominations with one win from 1971 through 1999.* • Placido Domingo receives his first nomination, for La Voce D'Oro *in Best Classical Vocal Soloist Performance. He will get his first win 10 years later for Verdi's La Traviata (with others in Best Opera Recording, where it tied with Mozart's Le Nozzi Di Figaro). Domingo will receive 29 nominations with 7 wins to date.*

# 17th Annual Grammy Awards

URIS THEATER, NEW YORK

*Eligibility Year: October 16, 1973–October 15, 1974*
*Announced on March 1, 1975*

*There was* a lot to honestly love about the 17th Annual Grammy Awards, and not just because wholesome heartthrob Olivia Newton-John won both Record of the Year and Best Pop Vocal Performance, Female, for "I Honestly Love You." This fifth live Grammy telecast was an extremely lively and often surprising affair. Returning host Andy Williams started off the night by joking about the then exploding number of new award shows, but almost immediately the night reminded viewers why the Grammy Awards are a show like no other.

It's safe to say no other awards telecast would have Roberta Flack announce, back to back, that pretelecast winners included Sebastian Cabot, Sterling Holloway, and Paul Winchell's *Winnie the Pooh and Tigger Too* (Best Recording for Children) and Richard Pryor's *That Nigger's Crazy* (Best Comedy Recording). None would have featured Aretha Franklin and the Righteous Brothers soulfully singing the nominations in presenting Best R&B Vocal Performance by a Duo, Group or Chorus; or David Essex and Sarah Vaughan vocalizing jazzily together; or Rudy Vallee and Paul Williams managing to share some funny megaphone patter. And where else would you have Bad Company and Graham Central Station compete with Marvin Hamlisch for Best New Artist?

And yet once again, Music's Biggest Night proved big enough to make it all fit together perfectly, thanks to one common link—the love and joy of music. For instance, when Hamlisch won Best New Artist, he immediately charmed the crowd by declaring "The really new artist of the year, I'm happy to say, is really Scott Joplin"—a reference to the late great ragtime legend whose music Hamlisch had used so effectively for the score to the box-office smash *The Sting*. "I'm just very happy that we were able ... to have the rest of you all hear what we had heard and really loved."

There were numerous performances to love on this Grammy night, from the Spinners taking "Mighty Love" to church to Harry Chapin making his Grammy debut as a nominee and performer playing "Cat's in the Cradle" with orchestral backing. "Putting 50 pieces behind me tonight is like putting a Rolls Royce engine in a flat bed truck," Chapin said with a charming grin, "but I'll do my best."

Left page:
*Stevie Wonder*
This page: *Paul Simon
and Art Garfunkel*

**WINNER SNAPSHOT**
**Record of the Year**
"I Honestly Love You" • Olivia Newton-John
**Album of the Year**
*Fulfillingness' First Finale* • Stevie Wonder
**Song of the Year**
"The Way We Were" • Alan Bergman, Marilyn Bergman &
Marvin Hamlisch, songwriters

**Best New Artist**
Marvin Hamlisch

Yet let there be no doubt about who gave an astonishingly riveting performance on this night—and clearly one of the most vital and pointed Grammy performances in its first 50 years. Still in the middle of one of the greatest Grammy rolls of all-time, the magnificent Stevie Wonder had everyone in the audience, from Marvin Hamlisch to the Pips, clapping in time to perhaps his most political and angry masterpiece ever, "You Haven't Done Nothin'"—a song that spoke powerfully to the climate of the mid-'70s in the inner cities. Ultimately, Wonder would add several more Grammys to his grand total this night—Album of the Year and Best Pop Vocal Performance, Male (both for *Fulfillingness' First Finale*), Best R&B Vocal Performance, Male ("Boogie on Reggae Woman"), and Best Rhythm & Blues Song ("Living for the City" from *Innervisions*). And for good measure, he also just happened to write "Tell Me Something Good," which won Rufus the Grammy for Best R&B Performance by a Duo, Group or Chorus.

Other great performances at the 17th Grammy Awards show included Aretha Franklin singing "Ain't Nothing Like the Real Thing," for which the Queen of Soul won Best R&B Vocal Performance, Female, an award presented to her by a then otherworldly David Bowie, who memorably explained, "Ladies and gentlemen, and others, I am honored to have been selected to perform this particular task. My personal award is having the opportunity to salute *ce premiere femme noir*." Accepting the Grammy, Franklin proclaimed, "Wow, this is so good I could kiss David Bowie. I mean that in a beautiful way because we did."

And yet that wasn't even the most remarkable presentation of the night, nor was Bette Midler presenting Stevie Wonder wearing a 45 rpm record of the Del Vikings' "Come and Go with Me" as her hat. No, that honor was reserved for the last award of the night, Record of the Year, for which the unlikely power trio of Paul Simon, John Lennon, and Andy Williams teamed up for some surreal but entertaining comedy referring to all of their former partners—Art Garfunkel, Paul McCartney, and Claudine Longet—with the former Beatle in particular coming off as simultaneously charming and mocking. Memorably, when an absent Olivia Newton-John won the award for "I Honestly Love You," Art Garfunkel—wearing a faux tux-T-shirt for the occasion—was chosen to accept on her behalf. "I thought I told you to wait in the car," Simon quipped. Garfunkel also got in a great jab, asking Simon, "Still writing, Paul?"

Ironically, while an absent Paul McCartney won a Grammy at the 17th Annual Grammy Awards (Best Pop Performance by a Duo, Group or Chorus for *Band on the Run*), this should go down as an extremely winning night for the very present John Lennon, too.

Left page clockwise from top left: *The Spinners • Aretha Franklin and David Bowie • David Bowie, Art Garfunkel, Paul Simon, Yoko Ono, John Lennon, and Roberta Flack* This page: *Harry Chapin*

*Did You Know …?* Stevie Wonder beats out a particularly rich Album of the Year field that includes *John Denver's* Back Home Again, *Elton John's* Caribou, *Paul McCartney and Wings'* Band on the Run, *and Joni Mitchell's* Court and Spark. • *Joni Mitchell is recognized with six nominations for* Court and Spark *and the single "Help Me," but wins only once, for Best Arrangement Accompanying Vocalist for "Down to You," which she shares with Tom Scott.* • *Mike Oldfield wins as composer of "Tubular Bells" (from* The Exorcist*) in Best Instrumental Composition.* • *Jazz great Charlie Parker has his only win. It is for* First Recordings! *in Best Jazz Performance by a Soloist.*

# 18th Annual Grammy Awards

*Eligibility Year: October 16, 1974–October 15, 1975*
*Announced on February 28, 1976*

*Held during* a year of widespread disco dancing, wide lapels, and bicentennial celebration, the 18th Annual Grammy Awards were hosted for the sixth time by Andy Williams. By this time, Williams was beginning to express a few complaints—albeit completely comedic ones—for his monologue. "Although I've never won anything ... one should not have to pay for one's own parking, or share one's dressing room with the Captain & Tennille's bulldogs." And in one of his racier lines, Williams also noted that the Grammy Awards were now 18 years old, adding, "So you can now take your Grammy across state lines without violating the Mann Act."

True to Williams' promise that "we'll be opening more envelopes than the CIA," the show got down to business following a rousing first performance of "This Will Be (An Everlasting Love)" by Natalie Cole (which would win Best R&B Vocal Performance, Female). Presenters Helen Reddy and Neil Sedaka then revealed that Cole had won the Grammy Award for Best New Artist. Before handing out the award for Best Jazz Performance by a Group—won by Chick Corea & Return to Forever—jazz vocal giants Ella Fitzgerald and Mel Tormé offered one of the evening's most spontaneous and winning performances with a master class in scatting. Academy President Jay Cooper then introduced Henry Mancini, who narrated a tribute to the music of the Windy City, Chicago—from its rich legacy in the blues to classical. Celebrating the music of Academy Chapter cities would be a theme from 1976 through 1979, with Atlanta, Memphis, and San Francisco saluted in addition to Chicago.

Producer and director Marty Pasetta peppered the 18th Grammy broadcast with a series of

**Left page:**
*The Muppets' Bert & Ernie (nominated for Best Recording for Children for Jim Henson and Sam Pottle)*
**This page:** *Natalie Cole*

---

**WINNER SNAPSHOT**
**Record of the Year**
"Love Will Keep Us Together" • Captain & Tennille
**Album of the Year**
*Still Crazy After All These Years* • Paul Simon
**Song of the Year**
"Send in the Clowns" • Stephen Sondheim, songwriter
**Best New Artist**
Natalie Cole

psychedelic graphic effects that made even Ray Stevens' rendition of "Misty" feel a little trippy. Indeed, there was something nice and trippy about a year in which Stephen Sondheim won Song of the Year for his Broadway ballad "Send in the Clowns," while the Best Pop Instrumental Performance Grammy went to Van McCoy for "The Hustle." Disco also emerged victorious in the Best R&B Instrumental Performance category, where Silver Convention's "Fly, Robin, Fly" rose to the occasion. With wins in both pop and R&B categories, disco was starting to show the short-lived hold it would soon have on the music world. Meanwhile, the ever-soulful Earth, Wind & Fire won their first

Grammy in the Best R&B Vocal Performance by a Duo, Group or Chorus category for "Shining Star." That award was handed out by Aretha Franklin and the Lockers, the funky dance troupe who gave the watching world a little disco lesson.

But this was also a fine night for members of the '70s singer/songwriter movement. Paul Simon, a defining figure in that genre, won Album of the Year and Best Pop Vocal Performance, Male, for his work on *Still Crazy After All These Years*. Janis Ian won Best Pop Vocal Performance, Female, for her confessional ballad "At Seventeen," while Larry Alexander, Brooks Arthur, and Russ Payne were awarded the Best Engineered Recording—Non-Classical for Ian's album *Between the Lines*. Another singer/songwriter on the show was a white-tuxedoed Barry Manilow, who performed a crowd-pleasing version of "Mandy," weaving in a bit of "Could It Be Magic" for good mellow measure.

Duos of various sorts also fared well at this Grammy show. Kris Kristofferson and Rita Coolidge won Best Country Vocal Performance by a Duo or Group for "Lover Please," and the Captain & Tennille took home the Grammy for Record of the Year for their debut pop smash "Love Will Keep Us Together."

But ultimately, the most charming thank you of the night came from Paul Simon, who earlier performed "50 Ways to Leave Your Lover" from a small platform in the audience. Accepting the Grammy Award for Album of the Year, Simon thanked a list of people that included his producer Phil Ramone and onetime partner Art Garfunkel. In the end, Simon got a tremendous laugh by concluding, "Most of all, I'd like to thank Stevie Wonder, who didn't make an album this year."

Left page clockwise from top left: *Janis Ian • Barry Manilow • Joan Baez, Stevie Wonder, and Captain & Tennille • Nominees Waylon Jennings and Jessi Colter* This page: *Ella Fitzgerald and Mel Tormé*

*Did You Know ...?* The Recording Academy adds the Best Latin Recording category. *Eddie Palmieri wins for* Sun of Latin Music. *• Willie Nelson receives his first win, for "Blue Eyes Crying in the Rain" in Best Country Vocal Performance, Male. He will receive 43 nominations with 6 wins to date.*

# 19th Annual Grammy Awards

HOLLYWOOD PALLADIUM, HOLLYWOOD

*Eligibility Year: October 16, 1975–September 30, 1976*
*Announced on February 19, 1977*

*After announcing* that the 19th Annual Grammy Awards marked his seventh time as host of the show, Andy Williams told the audience at the Hollywood Palladium, "I'm very proud of this Academy. There aren't many institutions that would go to so much time and care just to throw an annual get-together for Stevie Wonder." Williams then explained that Wonder would not be in the audience tonight, but would instead appear by satellite from Lagos, Nigeria.

Indeed, this would be the most global Grammy show yet, as it was transmitted via satellite to Hong Kong and the Far East. "I can just picture a Chinese family sitting in front of their television set with their chopsticks in hand watching all this silver and all this glitter and singing a gospel song along with the Oak Ridge Boys," Williams noted.

That Chinese family would have heard Best

Gospel Performance winners the Oak Ridge Boys sing the nominations in the category of Best Inspirational Performance—a category presented on air for the first time and won by Gary S. Paxton. They would have also witnessed a wide range of notable performances from the likes of Natalie Cole ("Mr. Melody"), Sarah Vaughan ("Tenderly"), Chet Atkins and Les Paul ("Deed I Do" from their album *Chester & Lester*, which won the Best Country Instrumental Award), and Barry Manilow, who performed "I Write the Songs," which had already won Song of the Year earlier in the evening for songwriter Bruce Johnston. Arguably, Manilow also should have been presented a special Grammy for Biggest Bow Tie.

The Starland Vocal Band, who won Best New Artist over competition that included Boston, the Brothers Johnson, Dr. Buzzard's Original Savannah

*Left page:*
*Barry Manilow*
*This page: Starland*
*Vocal Band*

**WINNER SNAPSHOT**
**Record of the Year**
"This Masquerade" • George Benson
**Album of the Year**
*Songs in the Key of Life* • Stevie Wonder
**Song of the Year**
"I Write the Songs" • Bruce Johnston, songwriter
**Best New Artist**
Starland Vocal Band

**SPECIAL MERIT AWARDS**
Trustees Award
Thomas A. Edison, Leopold Stokowski

Band, and white funk band Wild Cherry, performed "Afternoon Delight." This remains a relatively rare instance of a folky foursome paying a musical tribute to midday sexual interludes while backed by an orchestra.

One performance that was hard to see and barely heard because of a technical malfunction was Stevie Wonder's performance of "Sir Duke" from his *Songs in the Key of Life* album. After considerable buildup, the remote performance ended up illustrating the risk of going global. Indeed, Neil Armstrong's performance from the moon eight years earlier was transmitted more clearly. Nevertheless, it was another good Grammy night for Wonder who won Album of the Year; Best Pop Vocal Performance, Male; Best R&B Vocal Performance, Male; and Best Producer of the Year.

Other big winners for artistic achievement in America's bicentennial year included George Benson, who won three Grammys, including Record of the Year for his breakthrough hit "This Masquerade" and Best Pop Instrumental Performance for his *Breezin'* album. Benson also got to team up with a characteristically witty

Richard Pryor to present the Grammy for Best Jazz Vocal Performance to no less a legend than Ella Fitzgerald for *Fitzgerald and Pass ... Again*.

Other notable presenters included Gladys Knight & the Pips, who offered a salute to one of The Academy's chapter cities—Atlanta—that even included a little "Midnight Train to Georgia."

Ringo Starr and Paul Williams had a great deal of fun presenting the Grammy for Best Pop Vocal Performance, Female, to Linda Ronstadt for *Hasten Down the Wind*. The pair tap danced their way to the podium, where Starr said of the diminutive Williams, "Well, they promised me Paul Newman and look what I got." And best of all was Bette Midler, who helped turn the mood around after Wonder's performance from a distance didn't pan out. After wrapping part of what looked to be the 100-foot train of her dress around her head and declaring herself "The Ghost of Grammys Past," the Divine Miss M noted, "It's always nice to visit L.A.—the home of absolutely nothing. Except, of course, the music business—a business in which you are only as good as your last two minutes and 42 seconds."

Left page clockwise from top left: *Richard Pryor and George Benson* • *Peter Frampton* • *Wild Cherry* This page: *Chet Atkins, Dolly Parton, Freddy Fender, and Les Paul*

*Did You Know ...?* *The bicentennial year marked by the eligibility period for this Grammy show also happened to coincide with the 100th anniversary of the invention of sound recording. The Postmaster General took the opportunity of the 19th Grammy Awards to unveil a postage stamp commemorating the milestone.* • *Chicago gets its first and only win, for "If You Leave Me Now" in Best Pop Vocal Performance by a Duo, Group or Chorus.* • *Opera great Beverly Sills wins her only Grammy, for* Music of Victor Herbert *in Best Classical Vocal Soloist Performance.* • *The soundtrack for the urban farce* Car Wash *wins Album of Best Original Score Written for a Motion Picture or Television Special for Motown-affiliated composer Norman Whitfield. It tops scores by Dave Grusin* (Three Days of the Condor), *Bernard Hermann* (Taxi Driver), *and Jack Nitzsche* (One Flew Over the Cuckoo's Nest), *among others.*

SHRINE AUDITORIUM, LOS ANGELES

*Eligibility Year: October 1, 1976–September 30, 1977*
*Announced on February 23, 1978*

*Throughout* the 20th Annual Grammy Awards, a suitably far-flung galaxy of stars—quite literally from Queen of Soul Aretha Franklin to stoner comedy stars Cheech & Chong—appeared via videotape to wish the Grammys a happy 20th birthday. This wasn't the only significant nod to the show's illustrious past. In fact, the entire evening—hosted for the first time by John Denver, in an appropriately ruffled '70s tux—kicked off with an extended overture that found a troupe of interpretive dancers doing their thing to the soundtrack of all 19 past winners for Record of the Year.

Yet the first live musical performance of the night was very much of the moment as teen idol and Best New Artist nominee Shaun Cassidy, dressed in an all-white pantsuit, kicked things into gear with a surprisingly convincing rendition of "That's Rock & Roll." Yet when Steve Martin—already a winner for Best Comedy Recording for *Let's Get Small*—and Chicago came together to present the Best New Artist, the award went instead to Debby Boone, Pat Boone's

daughter, who was riding the crest of her success with the smash ballad "You Light Up My Life."

"You Light Up My Life" also won Song of the Year in a rare Grammy tie with "Love Theme from *A Star Is Born* (Evergreen)" by Barbra Streisand and Paul Williams. For his part, the witty Williams made one of the more memorable Grammy acceptance speeches by thanking by name a physician for providing him with "some incredible Valium that got me through the entire experience." Joe Brooks, who wrote "You Light Up My Life," then delivered one of the other memorable lines of the night when he pointed out that many of the music professionals in attendance had actually turned down his song, some of them multiple times, before adding, "This tastes so sweet."

In accepting the Grammy for Best Pop Vocal Performance, Female, earlier in the evening, Streisand seemed genuinely taken aback to have triumphed over Linda Ronstadt, Dolly Parton, Carly Simon, and Debby Boone. "Gee, I'm really surprised," she told the

*Left page from top:*
*Crosby, Stills & Nash*
*present the Album of the*
*Year Grammy to Fleetwood*
*Mac • Shaun Cassidy*
*This page: George Benson,*
*Natalie Cole and Lou Rawls*

**WINNER SNAPSHOT**
**Record of the Year**
"Hotel California" • Eagles
**Album of the Year**
*Rumours* • Fleetwood Mac
**Song of the Year** (Tie)
"Love Theme from *A Star Is Born* (Evergreen)"
• Barbra Streisand & Paul Williams, songwriters
"You Light Up My Life" • Joe Brooks, songwriter

**Best New Artist**
Debby Boone

crowd. "I know I won four Grammys, but I didn't remember for what because it was such a long time ago." Indeed, Streisand had last won at the 8th Annual Grammy Awards show in 1966.

This was a night full of varied presenters, including legends Minnie Pearl (who charmingly contended that staring into John Denver's eyes had given her a "Rocky Mountain High") and Cab Calloway (who seemed genuinely taken aback by a big reaction from the crowd, telling them, "Thank you—and I'm so glad you remembered"). The only genre conspicuously absent was punk rock, which had just hit Mother England during the previous year. There were also notable performances from the sublime— Count Basie and his band performing "Sweet Georgia Brown"—to the sublimely ridiculous—soul great Joe Tex performing "Ain't Gonna Bump No More (With No Big Fat Woman)" with the help of an unusually voluptuous bumping and grinding dancer.

The always amiable John Denver, who had recently starred along with comedy great George Burns in the smash film *Oh, God!*, kept his own quips to a minimum on this Grammy night. Early on, however, he did gamely report that, because space backstage was at a premium, artists had to share dressing rooms by genre. "I am personally sharing my dressing room with Dolly Parton and Emmylou Harris," he explained with an unusually lusty grin. "Thank God *I'm* a country boy." Denver would ultimately host the show five more times, becoming, like Andy Williams before him, a sort of Grammy regular. Remarkably, Denver would not actually win a Grammy himself until shortly after his death in 1997.

In the end, this 20th anniversary show was a Grammy night that found The Academy recognizing many of the finest and most popular recording artists on the West Coast rock scene, with the Eagles winning Record of the Year for "Hotel California," Fleetwood Mac taking Album of the Year for *Rumours*, and Steely Dan's *Aja* taking home the award for Best Engineered Recording—Non-Classical. The force was also with John Williams, who won the Grammy for Best Original Score Written for a Motion Picture or a Television Special and Best Instrumental Composition for his music for *Star Wars*.

While presenting the Album of the Year award to Fleetwood Mac, Graham Nash looked at his copresenters David Crosby and Stephen Stills and posed perhaps one of the most thoughtful questions in Grammy history— one that subtly spoke to the wonderful culture clash that was the Grammy Awards at age 20: "Does anybody have any idea what it took to get Crosby into a tuxedo?"

Left page clockwise from top: *Andy Gibb and Stephen Bishop • Debby Boone • Steve Martin • Crystal Gayle • Paul Williams* This page: *Cab Calloway*

*Did You Know ...?* *The Commodores earn their first nomination with "Easy" in Best R&B Vocal Performance by a Duo, Group, or Chorus. (As a group member, this would also be Lionel Richie's first nomination.)* • *The Bee Gees win their first Grammy for "How Deep Is Your Love" in the Best Pop Vocal Performance by a Group category.* • *Crystal Gayle takes home her only Grammy with her win in Best Country Vocal Performance, Female, for "Don't It Make My Brown Eyes Blue."*

# 21st Annual Grammy Awards

"I *look* out here at all the members of The Recording Academy and I see a lot of silks and satins and jewelry and new hair styles—and gee, the ladies look fantastic, too," host John Denver (wearing a tux with bell-bottom pants) said with a smile at the start of the 21st Annual Grammy Awards show, the last ceremony held in the '70s. Indeed, the music industry really was growing up in a number of fascinating ways. "Twenty-one is a very special age," Denver noted. "Twenty-one is when you come of age." Among those coming along for the ride on this Grammy night were winners from A Taste of Honey of "Boogie Oogie Oogie" fame—who won Best New Artist, beating out the likes of Elvis Costello, the Cars, Chris Rea, and Toto—to legendary pianist Vladimir Horowitz who received two classical awards. Where else in the world besides on the Grammys would Johnny "Take This Job and Shove It" Paycheck and the great tenor Jan Peerce be found next to each other on the bill?

Disco had very much come of age as Grammy 21 intermittently turned into Studio 54. The entrenchment of disco by 1978 had become a cultural phenomenon. Manhattan's Studio 54 was the most high-profile nightspot in the country; *Saturday Night Fever* took the nation's theaters by storm; and artists of all stripes—including such venerable rock acts as the Rolling Stones and Rod Stewart—were recording disco and releasing 12-inch club mixes. Disco colored the fashions (all those satins and silks Denver referred to in his opening remarks) and sense of the times, and the craze led to Denver awkwardly (though endearingly) appropriating John Travolta's *Fever* dance moves for his performance of the Bee Gees' "Stayin' Alive" during a tribute to the year's Song of the Year nominees. Perhaps not surprisingly, the Album of the Year Grammy was bestowed upon the smash hit *Saturday Night Fever* soundtrack.

The first performance of the night was the glitzy ode to the disco lifestyle "I Love the Nightlife" by Alicia Bridges. Dionne Warwick and Quincy Jones presented the Grammy award for Best R&B Vocal Performance, Female, to Donna Summer—who faced considerable competition from nominees such as Aretha Franklin, Natalie Cole, Chaka Khan, and Bridges herself—for "Last Dance."

Left page: *Steve Martin*
This page: *Chuck Mangione*

**WINNER SNAPSHOT**
**Record of the Year**
"Just the Way You Are" • Billy Joel
**Album of the Year**
*Saturday Night Fever—Soundtrack* • Various Artists
**Song of the Year**
"Just the Way You Are" • Billy Joel, songwriter
**Best New Artist**
A Taste of Honey

**SPECIAL MERIT AWARDS**
Trustees Award
Goddard Lieberson, Frank Sinatra

101

In the midst of the discothon, the Grammys managed to do what it always does best—highlight all kinds of music, including Chuck Mangione's flugelhorn hit "Feels So Good" and a rousing number by Oscar Peterson, winner of Best Jazz Instrumental Performance, Soloist (*Montreaux '77—Oscar Peterson Jam*).

In addition to Johnny Paycheck's biting state of the working man performance, country music was well represented by presenters who spoke their minds. Before announcing that his future fellow Highwayman Willie Nelson had won the Grammy for Best Country Vocal Performance, Male ("Georgia on My Mind"), Kris Kristofferson, with wife Rita Coolidge at his side, told the crowd, "I think there ought to be a special award given every year to George Jones and Jerry Lee

Lewis just for being who they are." Glen Campbell and then flame Tanya Tucker did a very special picking and singing presentation of the award for Best Country Vocal Performance by a Duo or Group that became a little more special when it turned out that neither of the beloved country outlaws Waylon Jennings nor Willie Nelson was there to pick up the award for the now-iconic "Mamas Don't Let Your Babies Grow Up to Be Cowboys." "Well, as most of you know, Waylon and Willie wouldn't walk a mile to see a pissant eat a bale of hay, but we congratulate them anyway and accept it on their behalf," Campbell said.

And perhaps in a moment of nostalgia for some old-fashioned rock, The Academy recognized Steely Dan's "FM (No Static At All)"—from the movie celebrating the age of free-form radio—with a Best Engineered Recording, Non-Classical, for Roger Nichols and Al Schmitt.

Another of the evening's big winners was also not in attendance—Billy Joel, who won both Record of the Year for "Just the Way You Are" along with his producer Phil Ramone, and Song of the Year for the same classic romantic ballad. Barry Manilow definitely was there to pick up his only Grammy to date for Best Pop Vocal Performance, Male, for "Copacabana (At The Copa)." And if the experience wasn't memorable enough, Manilow received his award from Steve Martin—winner of the Best Comedy Recording for *A Wild and Crazy Guy*—who took the stage in a tux with no pants, which were later handed to him in dry-cleaner wrapping. Martin went on to offer his own memorable thanks, including a shout out to his own manager "who has believed in me ever since the first album started selling."

The most inspiring performer of the night, however, may have been 96-year-old Eubie Blake, who would arguably have been named Best New Artist of 1921 had there been a Grammy Awards then. Blake performed his classic "I'm Just Wild About Harry," with dancing girls several generations his junior, and then presented the Best New Artist award with Denver. "Boy," Blake said with a youthful smile on his face, "I'm having the time of my life up here."

Left page clockwise from top left:
*John Denver* • *Al Jarreau* • *Olivia Newton-John* • *Alicia Bridges*
This page:
*Bee Gees*

*Did You Know …?* Luciano Pavarotti wins his first Grammy Award, for Luciano Pavarotti: Hits from Lincoln Center. • Billy Joel's wins for Record and Song of the Year are also his first ever nominations. • Saturday Night Fever *produces the most Grammy statuettes ever given out in one category. Fifty Grammys are awarded for this one Album of the Year win to the various artists and producers who worked on the record.*

# 1980s

As it turns out, video actually *didn't* kill the radio star.

Yet with the pastel-colored dawn of the MTV age in the '80s, the popular music

world did take on a visibly shinier new surface. As always, the Grammy Awards

reflected its times during an era that introduced such innovations as the Walkman, the

compact disc, the explosion of the personal computer, Donkey Kong, and Reaganomics. The '80s were also marked by increasingly large-scale and ambitious Grammy shows as well as by some notably winning years for recording artists that included everyone from Christopher Cross to Michael Jackson to Toto to Bonnie Raitt.

# 22nd Annual Grammy Awards

SHRINE AUDITORIUM, LOS ANGELES
*Eligibility Year: October 1, 1978–September 30, 1979*
*Announced on February 27, 1980*

*No, Neil* Diamond didn't bring Barbra Streisand flowers—at least not onstage—but the former schoolmates from Erasmus High in Brooklyn did make Grammy history together at the 22nd Annual Grammy Awards.

The two superstars came together for the first time to perform "You Don't Bring Me Flowers," the song that became an accidental smash duet when an enterprising disc jockey spliced together Diamond and Streisand's separate but equally winning recordings. For all the heartbreak of the song's lyrics, this brilliant summit meeting would end in hugs, a kiss, and one of the most enthusiastic audience reactions in Grammy history.

For all that, despite two nominations, "You Don't Bring Me Flowers" did not win any Grammy Awards. Yet, as host Kenny Rogers explained in his monologue, the Grammy was now more than ever a true object of desire. "We are entering the second decade of our Grammy Award shows on television—and we've all come a long way since the first time. And today the Grammy is finally established in the minds of everyone as the most meaningful and highly desired award."

Among those enjoying a particularly meaningful and memorable night were the Doobie Brothers, who won Record of the Year for "What a Fool Believes," as well as Best Pop Vocal Performance by a Duo, Group, or Chorus for *Minute by Minute*, while "What a Fool Believes" also prevailed in the Song of the Year category for writers Michael McDonald and Kenny Loggins. Michael Jackson also won his first Grammy (Best R&B Vocal Performance, Male, for "Don't Stop 'Til You Get Enough"), and Bob Dylan won his second—Best Rock Vocal Performance, Male, for "Gotta Serve Somebody."

Left page: *Neil Diamond and Barbra Streisand*
This page: *Rickie Lee Jones*

**WINNER SNAPSHOT**
**Record of the Year**
"What a Fool Believes" • The Doobie Brothers
**Album of the Year**
*52nd Street* • Billy Joel
**Song of the Year**
"What a Fool Believes" • Kenny Loggins & Michael McDonald, songwriters
**Best New Artist**
Rickie Lee Jones

Dylan's performance of the song was the best sort of fire-and-brimstone rock gospel—a religious *and* musical experience in the best possible way. Billy Joel won Album of the Year and Best Pop Vocal Performance, Male, for his work on *52nd Street*.

This was also a memorable night for fine female singers of assorted vintage. The dynamic duo of Debbie Harry and George Burns presented Rickie Lee Jones with the Best New Artist Grammy—Jones' unusually humorous group of fellow nominees were the Blues Brothers and Robin Williams, as well as breakout bands the Knack and Dire Straits. Meanwhile, veteran songstress Dionne Warwick marked a significant comeback, winning her first Grammys in nearly a decade. She won the awards for Best Pop Vocal Performance, Female, for "I'll Never Love This Way Again"—which she also performed on the show with characteristic grace—as well as Best R&B Vocal Performance, Female, for "Déjà Vu." A thrilled Warwick told the audience, "My grandpa told me a long time ago 'to those who wait good things do come.' I thank you for waiting."

There was no shortage of star power in the house for this Grammy Awards telecast. Charlie Daniels opened the show with his Grammy-winning "The Devil Went Down to Georgia," despite having broken his arm in five places (fiddle greats Vassar Clements and Buddy Spicher rosined up the bows while Daniels sang). Vocal legends and nominees Sarah Vaughan and Joe Williams represented the jazz contingent in style with their medley of "The Face I Love" and "When You're Smiling." And though not winners this night, Sister Sledge was as hot an act as any after the recent world champion Pittsburgh Pirates had adopted "We Are Family" as their theme song. The Sisters turned in a vibrant performance of their hit.

And for country royalty, Johnny Cash and June Carter playfully presented the first two awards of the night—both country awards. Before doing so, Carter spoke about the global reach of country music and recalled hearing Cash's records playing in Israel during their honeymoon. "Is that *all* you remember about our honeymoon?" the Man in Black memorably asked—a quarter-century before Cash and Carter's dramatic love story was brought to life on the big screen with *Walk the Line*.

Left page clockwise from top left: *Bob Dylan • Debbie Harry and George Burns • Johnny Cash and June Carter • Sarah Vaughan and Joe Williams* This page: *Kenny Loggins (center) with the Doobie Brothers*

*Did You Know ...?* Gloria Gaynor's classic "I Will Survive" wins the Best Disco Recording category. Reflecting the genre's quick burn, the category was eliminated the following year, making Gaynor the only winner. • Latin legend Celia Cruz (with Johnny Pacheco) earns her first Grammy nomination for the album Eternos in Best Latin Recording.

# 23rd Annual Grammy Awards

RADIO CITY MUSIC HALL, NEW YORK

*Eligibility Year: October 1, 1979–September 30, 1980*
*Announced on February 25, 1981*

The first Grammy show honoring the music of the '80s (and the first ever held at New York's famed Radio City Music Hall) was hosted by one of the most important singer/songwriters of the '60s and '70s, and all the years that have followed for that matter—Paul Simon. After slyly telling the Radio City crowd that both of his parents were Rockettes, Simon said, "I am very happy to be here. It's not only a great honor to be asked, but I think it's a very nice career move as well."

Yet starting with the first award of the night presented on air, Best New Artist, it became clear that this night would belong, award-wise at least, to another singer/songwriter—a previously less-heralded artist named Christopher Cross. At the time, Cross was enjoying tremendous success with his 1980 debut album that featured such smashes as "Sailing," "Ride Like the Wind," and "Never Be the Same." And by the end of this Grammy night, the soft-spoken Texan would pick up five Grammy Awards, including the so-called Big Four—Album of the Year, Record of the Year, Song of the Year, and Best New Artist. For the record, no artist thus far has repeated that achievement.

Standout performances varied widely on the show, from Irene Cara's opening rendition of "Fame," which started outside of Radio City and found the singer and dancers working their way down the aisle to the stage, to George Jones' short but heartbreaking rendition of the country classic "He Stopped Loving Her Today," which earned a Grammy for Best Country Vocal Performance, Male. The night also featured a multiracial gospel supergroup (including the Archers, Andrae Crouch, Reba Rambo, and B.J. Thomas) coming together to perform a kind of disco/gospel version of "The Lord's Prayer" and Chuck Mangione and the Manhattan Transfer jazzing things up together on a medley of "Birdland" and "Give It All You Got."

*Left page: Kenny Loggins performs "I'm Alright" with drummer Steve Gadd*
*This page: Christopher Cross and Michael Omartian*

**WINNER SNAPSHOT**
**Record of the Year**
"Sailing" • Christopher Cross
**Album of the Year**
*Christopher Cross* • Christopher Cross
**Song of the Year**
"Sailing" • Christopher Cross, songwriter
**Best New Artist**
Christopher Cross

**SPECIAL MERIT AWARDS**
Trustees Award
Count Basie, Aaron Copland

Appropriately enough, Paul Simon played the stirring "Late in the Evening" late in the evening and kept things moving along throughout in his own low-key and witty way. "Our next two presenters are not only great performers and legends in their own time, they're also well-known bigots and drug abusers," he announced at one point. Pausing for a big laugh, Simon then added, "I just wanted to say that as an introduction. Nobody ever gives that introduction actually."

An even bigger laugh came in response to presenters Barbra Streisand and Barry Gibb—winners in the Best Pop Performance by a Duo or Group with Vocal. Taking the stage, Streisand and Gibb, both dressed in white as on her hugely successful *Guilty* album cover, looked a little sheepish.

"Barry, do you feel guilty?" Streisand asked.

"No," Gibb told her shyly.

"No?" she said. "I do."

"Why?" Gibb asked her. "Why would you feel like that?"

"I don't know—I feel like I'm cheating on Neil Diamond," she said, referring to the man with whom she famously sang "You Don't Bring Me Flowers" on the 22nd Grammy Awards show.

The pair then presented Billy Joel with the Grammy for Best Rock Vocal Performance, Male, for his

*Glass Houses* album—a category in which his fellow nominees were Jackson Browne, Paul McCartney, Bruce Springsteen, and Kenny Loggins. Phil Ramone, who had produced recent efforts by both Billy Joel and Paul Simon, won Producer of the Year, Non-Classical.

In his acceptance speech, Ramone took time to thank "my little Ramones ... not the ones who make records—the other ones."

One innovative moment came at the end of the show. Many years before shows like MTV's *Unplugged* or VH1's *Story-tellers*, this Grammy show presented a group of songwriters nominated for Song of the Year—including Amanda McBroom ("The Rose"), Christopher Cross ("Sailing"), Fred Ebb and John Kander ("New York, New York"), Dean Pitchford and Michael Gore ("Fame"), and Lionel Richie ("Lady")—to both explain and perform stripped down versions of the songs. It was a vivid reminder of the power of the songwriter.

Finally, before closing the show, Paul Simon took the stage of Radio City to recall the impact of one of the greatest songwriters of all time—John Lennon, who had been killed outside New York's Dakota apartments only months prior to the show. As Simon put it simply and powerfully, "We'll miss his music, his humor, and his common sense."

Left page clockwise from top left: *Pat Benatar • Barry Gibb and Barbra Streisand • Irene Cara performs "Fame" • George Jones • Paul Simon* This page: *Billy Joel*

# 24th Annual Grammy Awards

SHRINE AUDITORIUM, LOS ANGELES
Eligibility Year: October 1, 1980–September 30, 1981
Announced on February 24, 1982

The opening list of talent for the 24th Annual Grammy Awards spoke to the musical and generational diversity of the show that would soon follow. After all, what other internationally televised event might conceivably and credibly bring together Carol Channing and Adam Ant? Ted Nugent and Ben Vereen? Rick James and Harry James? Only the Grammys—and only this one.

The winners, too, were decidedly diverse and multi-generational. Even though she was not present, this was a big night for the legendary Lena Horne— the recording from her big Broadway comeback *Lena Horne: The Lady and Her Music, Live on Broadway* won Best Pop Vocal Performance, Female, as well as Best Cast Show Album for its producer, Quincy Jones.

The 24th Grammy show would also be an exceptional evening for Jones, who chose to make Horne's album the very first release on his new Qwest Records

label. To top it off, Jones himself also won Best R&B Performance by a Duo or Group with Vocal for his album *The Dude*, as well as two separate Grammys for arranging on that album—one with Johnny Mandel (for "Velas") and the other with Jerry Hey (for "Ai No Corrida"). Meanwhile, Jones' protégé James Ingram, who gave the first performance of the night singing "Just Once" with Jones conducting, took home the Grammy for Best R&B Vocal Performance, Male, for "One Hundred Ways," which he sang on *The Dude*. Yet the highlight of the night for Jones was likely the experience of finally winning his first— but not last—Grammy as Producer of the Year. After a lengthy standing ovation, Jones explained with a big smile on his face, "Man, when I started waiting for this award I had long flowing hair and a thin waistline like James Ingram."

A new wind was blowing in the music industry:

Left page: *Quincy Jones*
This page: *Ted Nugent and Adam Ant*

**WINNER SNAPSHOT**
**Record of the Year**
"Bette Davis Eyes" • Kim Carnes
**Album of the Year**
*Double Fantasy* • John Lennon & Yoko Ono
**Song of the Year**
"Bette Davis Eyes" • Jackie DeShannon & Donna Weiss, songwriters

**Best New Artist**
Sheena Easton

MTV launched the previous year (August 1, 1981), and its influence could be seen on a number of winners who had enjoyed big videos along with big radio hits: "Bette Davis Eyes" won Record of the Year for its singer Kim Carnes and producer Val Garay and Song of the Year for its writers Jackie DeShannon and Donna Weiss; Rick Springfield won the Grammy for Best Rock Vocal Performance, Male, for "Jessie's Girl," triumphing over Bruce Springsteen, Rod Stewart, Rick James, and Gary U.S. Bonds; and the videogenic Sheena Easton was named the year's Best New Artist. In its debut year, the category of Video of the Year went to *Michael Nesmith in Elephant Parts*, a fitting award for the former star of *The Monkees*.

One of the night's breakout performances, however, came from a decidedly pre-MTV performer. As part of an uplifting gospel-themed segment also featuring the Reverend Al Green and the Archers, Joe Cocker took the stage to sing a lived-in version of "I'm So Glad I'm Standing Here Today" with the Crusaders—a standout track from that group's *Standing Tall* album. Cocker and the Crusaders did not win that award, but Cocker's heartfelt performance earned a tremendous ovation and later

helped inspire director Taylor Hackford to have Cocker sing what would be his comeback smash—"Up Where We Belong" with Jennifer Warnes for the soundtrack of *An Officer and a Gentleman*.

Another notable, and in this case suitably super freaky, performance came from Rick James, whom show host John Denver introduced thusly: "First there was rock. Then there was hard rock. Then there was punk rock, and now thanks mainly to our next performer, there's punk funk. You have to watch how you say that on television." The punk funk of James' "Give It To Me Baby" tore up the stage, with James himself taking turns at the drums and a nearly collapsing keyboard.

Yet there was little doubt that the most moving moment of the night came when the Grammy for Album of the Year was awarded to John Lennon and Yoko Ono's *Double Fantasy* album. "I really don't know what to say," said Ono, who was joined onstage by her and Lennon's young son Sean (as well as producer Jack Douglas). "I think John is here with us today. Both John and I were always very proud and happy that we were part of the human race. He made good music for the earth and for the universe." Indeed he did.

*Did You Know …? John Coltrane earns his only Grammy win, for "Bye Bye Blackbird" in Best Jazz Instrumental Performance, Soloist. • John Lennon receives his first solo nomination sans the Beatles or Paul McCartney.*

# 25th Annual Grammy Awards

SHRINE AUDITORIUM, LOS ANGELES

*Eligibility Year: October 1, 1981–September 30, 1982*
*Announced on February 23, 1983*

*To celebrate* Grammy's first quarter century, the 25th Annual Grammy Awards featured all the excitement of a big anniversary celebration … and Toto, too.

Toto—a musically accomplished group of top Los Angeles session musicians who received relatively little credit from the major rock press of the day—got some Grammy love this year, winning not only Record of the Year for their smash "Rosanna," but also Album of the Year for *Toto IV*, as well as Grammys for Best Instrumental Arrangement Accompanying Vocals to Jerry Hey and the group's David Paich and Jeff Porcaro and Best Vocal Arrangement for Two or More Voices to David Paich, both for the track "Rosanna." And in a surprisingly rare Grammy call out for a nay-saying rock critic, Paich got a laugh from the crowd by sarcastically acknowledging from the stage, "We'd like to thank Robert Hilburn for believing in us," when in fact the longtime *Los Angeles Times* rock critic had done absolutely nothing of the sort.

Still, the 25th Annual Grammy Awards were for the most part an appropriately positive affair. "This is a

milestone in the life of the Grammy Awards, and a celebration is definitely in order and in store," host John Denver explained, adding that "some of Grammy's greatest moments" from the past would be replayed throughout the night. Some new history was made on this Grammy night with an altogether remarkable live performance organized by then new Grammy producer Ken Ehrlich that featured Ray Charles, Count Basie, Jerry Lee Lewis, and Little Richard running through some of their greatest hits at four pianos—a true musical Fab Four for the ages. The ensemble started with Charles' "What'd I Say," then worked through Basie's "One O'Clock Jump," Lewis' "Whole Lotta Shakin' Goin' On," Little Richard's gospel-fueled "Joy, Joy, Joy," and Charles' "Wish You Were Here Tonight," before reprising "What'd I Say."

The second performance of the night found Joe Cocker and Jennifer Warnes dueting on "Up Where We Belong," their smash hit from the film *An Officer and a Gentleman*. This was a duet with a little Grammy history itself. Warnes had performed way back on the 11th

Left page: *Marvin Gaye*
This page: *Toto*

**WINNER SNAPSHOT**
**Record of the Year**
"Rosanna" • Toto
**Album of the Year**
*Toto IV* • Toto
**Song of the Year**
"Always on My Mind" • Wayne Carson, Johnny Christopher & Mark James, songwriters

**Best New Artist**
Men at Work
**SPECIAL MERIT AWARDS**
Trustees Award
Les Paul

Annual Grammy Awards' "The Best on Record" broadcast as part of the Los Angeles company of *Hair*, while Cocker's performance with the Crusaders at the 24th Annual Grammy Awards had helped inspire director Taylor Hackford to choose Cocker to sing "Up Where We Belong." Cocker and Warnes would then win the Grammy for Best Pop Performance by a Duo or Group with Vocal.

After some intelligent musical history offered by Recording Academy Chairman/President Bill Ivey, guitar pioneer Les Paul was presented with a Trustees Award. "I'm sorry that Mary isn't here to accept this with me," Paul said of his late great partner Mary Ford. "And I want to thank all the people that are watching on their radios."

Les Paul wasn't the only one getting in a good line. Eddie Murphy—who was all the rage on *Saturday Night Live* in 1982, the same year that would see his big-screen breakthrough in *48 Hrs.*—had some stand-up fun speaking about the tension of being nominated for a Grammy. "You know what's funny about this?" Murphy told the crowd. "A lot of people gonna lose tonight—and you got your tuxedos on and you're losing and it's *funny*." Murphy then pretended to not know that he himself had in fact lost Best Comedy Recording to Richard Pryor during the pretelecast and declared, "See, I *ain't* leaving here without a Grammy." Later, when Lionel Richie won the Grammy for Best Pop Vocal Performance, Male, for his early solo hit "Truly," Murphy got a standing ovation for

crashing the stage and temporarily relieving the former Commodore of his glittering prize. "Who *was* that masked man?" Richie joked. For the record, Murphy did in fact give the Grammy back.

At a quarter century, the Grammy Awards inevitably reflected popular music in the early '80s as MTV was just beginning to make its impact. The Best New Artist Grammy, for instance, went to early MTV favorites Men at Work, while the other nominees included early video stars the Stray Cats, Human League, and Asia, as well as Jennifer Holliday, who became a star from the original Broadway recording of *Dreamgirls*. Yet there was also a deep sense of history throughout the night, including a stunning R&B segment that featured an excellent run of performances from Harvey & The Moonglows, Gladys Knight & the Pips, the Spinners, and, finally, Marvin Gaye, who marked what would be his tragically short-lived comeback with a rousing and, yes, arousing rendition of "Sexual Healing"—for which he won two Grammys.

In a rare serious moment onstage, Eddie Murphy summed up the night and the state of the Grammys at 25. "You guys are not like doctors or nothing like that," he said, "but you're real important to people's lives because you give people's lives atmosphere ... I thank you for being what you are and keep kicking butt in the '80s." As Murphy said this, Grammy director Walter C. Miller cut wonderfully to a sprightly Ella Fitzgerald clapping along enthusiastically.

Left page clockwise from top: *Alabama* • *Henry Mancini, Eddie Murphy, Melissa Manchester, and Lionel Richie* • *Rick James and Grace Jones* • *Best Classical Vocal Soloist Performance winner Leontyne Price*
This page: *Linda Ronstadt*

*Did You Know ...?* Three of the night's nominees, Count Basie (who won), Ella Fitzgerald, and Henry Mancini, earned their first nominations and wins 25 years prior at the first awards presentation in 1958. • Marvin Gaye, shortly before his death, gets his only wins. They are for "Sexual Healing" in Best R&B Vocal Performance, Male, and for the instrumental version of "Sexual Healing" in Best R&B Instrumental Performance. • Mel Tormé has his first win, for An Evening with George Shearing and Mel Tormé in Best Jazz Vocal Performance, Male.

# 26th Annual Grammy Awards

As visionary as he may have been, George Orwell strangely did not write at all about the 26th Annual Grammy Awards in his classic novel *Nineteen Eighty-Four*. For better or worse, this Grammy show occurred not during utter domination by a totalitarian state, but rather during a year significantly dominated by the continuing rise of MTV and the record-breaking commercial impact of Michael Jackson.

John Denver—hosting his fifth show—wasted no time on a monologue, promising "a show so hot it's going to pop if we don't get right into it." Stressing that it had been an amazing year for women in music, he got right to the first performance of the night—Donna Summer singing "She Works Hard for the Money." Like so much of the rest of the telecast, Summer's opening performance—presented as a video-like production number—reflected the look and feel of music's new video age. In fact, throughout the evening nominees were announced with the help of extended video clips, as if audiences couldn't get enough of the videos that were now beginning to drive so much of the music business, commercially and artistically.

Denver then took the stage to explain that the big words of the past year had been "videos, Boy George, and Michael …," leaving the audience to loudly scream out "Jackson" with Jackson himself seated in the front row, where he would spend the night between his date Brooke Shields and diminutive *Webster* star Emmanuel Lewis, with producer Quincy Jones sitting nearby. This proved convenient, since Jackson and Jones would end up taking quite a few trips to the stage to accept Grammys during the next few hours.

The first award of the evening—Song of the Year, presented by esteemed authorities Stevie Wonder and Bob Dylan—did not go to Jackson for "Billie Jean" or "Beat It," but rather to Police chief Sting for "Every Breath You Take." The Police were on tour, but in their absence, Dylan announced, "We'll take it." The song would also win the Police a Grammy this night for Best Pop Performance by a Duo or Group with Vocal, and "Synchronicity" would win Best Rock Performance by a Duo or Group with Vocal—leaving copresenters Alice Cooper and Grace Jones to accept for them.

Joan Rivers and Culture Club were also not in the house, but appeared live from London via satellite, along with a Margaret Thatcher impersonator, to read the Grammy rules. Rivers wryly explained the reason for reviewing the rules:

*Left page: Annie Lennox*
*This page: Boy George*

**WINNER SNAPSHOT**
**Record of the Year**
"Beat It" • Michael Jackson
**Album of the Year**
*Thriller* • Michael Jackson
**Song of the Year**
"Every Breath You Take" • Sting, songwriter
**Best New Artist**
Culture Club

**SPECIAL MERIT AWARDS**
Lifetime Achievement Award
Chuck Berry, Charlie Parker

Trustees Award
Béla Bartók

"Every one of the nominees out there should know why they lost out to Michael Jackson." Rivers also informed Culture Club's gender-bending front man Boy George that he looked like "Brooke Shields on steroids." For his part, Boy George came off as a perfect, cross-dressing gentleman.

Explicitly paying tribute to music's new video age, John Denver noted that while music videos were nonexistent just a couple of years ago, they had "forged ahead to revitalize and totally reawaken the music industry." That said, an absent Duran Duran were awarded the first-ever Grammy for Best Video Album (*Duran Duran*), having already won the Best Video, Short Form, for "Girls on Film/Hungry Like a Wolf" earlier in the evening.

One outstanding performance put the spotlight on a founding rock father from well before the birth of video—Chuck Berry, who received a Lifetime Achievement Award, along with the late Charlie Parker. Since Berry was not late, but rather very much alive, he not only accepted the award, but also rocked the house with some of his past classics, aided by guitar slinging help from Stevie Ray Vaughan and George Thorogood.

Other notable performances, however, reflected the videogenic nature of '80s music, including Irene Cara's "Flashdance ... What a Feeling," which took home the Grammy for Best Pop Vocal Performance, Female, as the title song from the smash film that itself demonstrated Hollywood's reaction to MTV-like editing. Best New Artist nominees Eurythmics also made a vivid impression by

performing "Sweet Dreams (Are Made of This)" with Annie Lennox dressed as Elvis Presley, yet another moment in a night of exceptional cross-dressing. As Boy George memorably noted in his acceptance speech when Culture Club was named Best New Artist, "Thank you, America, you've got taste, style, and you know a good drag queen when you see one."

Another notable piece of history was acknowledged by then Academy President Michael Melvoin who, after holding up a vinyl record, produced a smaller, shinier object and announced excitedly to the world, "This is the new compact disc." The soon-to-be widespread CD had been introduced to consumers in the early '80s and was still dwarfed in sales by LPs and cassettes.

Ultimately, though, this night proved the beginning of the King of Pop's reign, so much so that Michael Jackson began inviting other people up from the audience to share the Grammy stage with him as he accepted awards—first his label boss Walter Yetnikoff and later his three sisters Rebbie, La Toya, and future Grammy winner Janet. "When something like this happens, you want those who are very dear to you up here with you," Jackson said. He also explained, having won his seventh award of the night—which he noted was a new record—he would now actually take his glasses off at the personal request of his friend Katharine Hepburn.

Appropriately, the night ended with Jackson winning his eighth and final Grammy of the night when "Beat It" was named Record of the Year. "I love all the girls in the balcony," Jackson declared to all the cheers from on high.

*Left page clockwise from top left: Herbie Hancock performs Best R&B Instrumental Performance winner "Rockit" • Wynton Marsalis • Rodney Dangerfield and Cyndi Lauper • Michael Jackson* **This page:** *Big Country vocalist Stuart Adamson*

*Did You Know ...?* Noted pop artist Robert Rauschenberg wins the Best Album Package Grammy for art directing the Talking Heads' Speaking in Tongues. • Wynton Marsalis wins in both jazz and classical categories. He wins for "Think of One" in Best Jazz Instrumental Performance, Soloist, and for "Haydn/L. Mozart/Hummel Trumpet Concertos" in Best Classical Performance, Instrumental Soloist or Soloists (with Orchestra). • More drag queens: Members of the cast of La Cage Aux Folles (Walter Charles and Jaime Ross) perform "I Am What I Am" from that show in full cross-dress.

# 27th Annual Grammy Awards

SHRINE AUDITORIUM, LOS ANGELES

*Eligibility Year: October 1, 1983–September 30, 1984*
*Announced on February 26, 1985*

*In the middle* of the 27th Annual Grammy Awards show, the legendary conductor and composer Leonard Bernstein wonderfully captured the best of the Grammy spirit during his acceptance of a Lifetime Achievement Award. "I am very happy tonight for music," he said. "And I'll be even happier and maybe even ecstatic if tonight can be a step toward the ultimate marriage of all kinds of music, because they are all one." As Bernstein noted, echoing a famous quote from Duke Ellington, "There is only good and there is bad."

This would be an exceptionally good night for Tina Turner, one of the more heartening comeback stories of the '80s. Rising to heights she had never achieved during the course of her career as the front woman of the Ike & Tina Turner Revue, Turner became a global superstar in her own right with the success of her *Private Dancer* album in 1984. On Grammy night, that comeback appeared more like a coronation, or perhaps a re-coronation, of one of

music's most royal figures. Turner's smash "What's Love Got to Do with It" scored awards for Record of the Year, Song of the Year, and Best Pop Vocal Performance, Female. Turner also won the Grammy for Best Rock Vocal Performance, Female, for "Better Be Good to Me."

Hosted by John Denver, the show opened with Huey Lewis & The News performing an a cappella version of Curtis Mayfield's "It's Alright" and then a rendition of their own smash "The Heart of Rock and Roll," which elevated pulse rates when dancers joined the band onstage.

The first award of the evening—for Best New Artist, presented by Ray Davies of the Kinks and performance artist Laurie Anderson—went to Cyndi Lauper, who was joined onstage for her acceptance by Hulk Hogan, who was wearing a white short-sleeved tux shirt, black leather pants, and a black bow tie. During her speech, Lauper, in her wonderful New York accent, expressed heartfelt

Left page: *Prince*
This page: *Dee Snider*

**WINNER SNAPSHOT**
**Record of the Year**
"What's Love Got to Do with It" • Tina Turner
**Album of the Year**
*Can't Slow Down* • Lionel Richie
**Song of the Year**
"What's Love Got to Do with It" • Terry Britten & Graham Lyle, songwriters

**Best New Artist**
Cyndi Lauper
**SPECIAL MERIT AWARDS**
Lifetime Achievement Award
Leonard Bernstein

Trustees Award
Eldridge R. Johnson

127

thanks to the World Wrestling Federation and Captain Lou Albano, making this a relatively rare moment of Grammy and WWF synergy.

Another truly '80s moment was the nod to electronic music that found the Grammys teaming up Thomas Dolby, Herbie Hancock, Howard Jones, and Stevie Wonder for a medley that included Dolby's "She Blinded Me with Science" and Hancock's "Rockit."

In addition to her awards, Turner also gave what was clearly one of the standout performances of the night. "She's been described as the woman God made to show other women how to dance in high-heeled shoes," Denver said by way of an introduction. Turner sounded and looked wonderful singing "What's Love Got to Do with It" in a shiny red dress and ten-foot hair, and the standing ovation afterward was truly thunderous. "I've been waiting for this opportunity for such a long time," Turner said in accepting her first award of the night, before paraphrasing from the godfather of soul. "I feel really good."

Yet one other act gave Turner a run for her money during the 27th Annual Grammy show. Introduced by Recording Academy President Michael Melvoin as "someone who's taken the

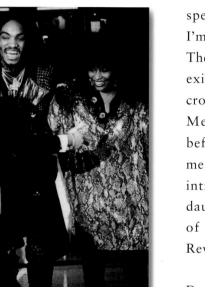

music world by storm," Prince—a winner for Best Rock Performance by a Duo or Group with Vocal and Best Album of Original Score Written for a Motion Picture or a Television Special, both for *Purple Rain*, and Best R&B Song for writing Chaka Khan's "I Feel for You"—took the stage to offer a breathless and spectacular version of "Baby, I'm a Star" that saw the Artist Then Still Known As Prince exiting shirtless through the crowd. Clearly a proud father, Melvoin took a moment beforehand to note, "It gives me extra added pleasure to introduce him because my daughter Wendy is a member of [Prince's band] the Revolution."

After a commercial break, Denver noted that in honor of Prince, he was wearing a purple cummerbund "hoping someone mistakes me for him. It didn't work."

But as brightly as Turner and Prince's stars were shining this night, opera singer Placido Domingo, himself a double winner on the evening, pointed out the Grammys' ability to transcend trends by spotlighting less obvious stars. "The big winner today," said Domingo in accepting the Best Opera Recording award, "is opera, because the award [is being presented] on television."

Left page clockwise from top left: *Tina Turner* • *Hank Williams Jr.,* • *"Weird Al" Yankovic wins Best Comedy Recording for* Eat It • *Herbie Hancock, Thomas Dolby, Stevie Wonder and Howard Jones* This page: *Melle Mel and Chaka Khan*

*Did You Know ...?* Lionel Richie's Can't Slow Down *takes the Grammy for Album of the Year against formidable competition:* Bruce Springsteen's Born in the U.S.A., *Tina Turner's* Private Dancer, *Prince and The Revolution's* Purple Rain, *and Cyndi Lauper's* She's So Unusual. • *The Best Reggae Recording category is added and won by Black Uhuru for* Anthem. • *Elizabeth Cotten becomes the oldest female to win a Grammy. At 90, she takes the Best Ethnic or Traditional Folk Recording for* Elizabeth Cotten Live!

# 28th Annual Grammy Awards

SHRINE AUDITORIUM, LOS ANGELES
*Eligibility Year: October 1, 1984–September 30, 1985*
*Announced on February 25, 1986*

*There was* no sign declaring "Check Your Ego at the Door" before the 28th Annual Grammy Awards ceremony, but USA for Africa, the historic all-star benefit for African relief, enjoyed Record of the Year, Song of the Year, Best Pop Performance by a Duo or Group with Vocal, and Best Music Video, Short Form, awards for "We Are the World." However, this wide-ranging Grammy show began on a different, more somber musical and political note with Sting appearing in a tux before an orchestra to perform his Cold War commentary "Russians," complete with its famous lyric, "I hope the Russians love their children too."

Host Kenny Rogers, turning out in a rhinestone tux, noted that the past year wasn't the first time the

music industry had expressed its social conscience, before introducing a performance by one of the artists who ruled the mid-'80s, Phil Collins. Soon after, James Taylor and Linda Ronstadt presented Collins with the Grammy Award for Best Pop Vocal Performance, Male, for his *No Jacket Required* album. Collins' other awards for the night were Album of the Year and Producer of the Year (with his then collaborator Hugh Padgham). Then Dionne Warwick—along with Julian Lennon—presented the Best Pop Vocal Performance, Female, to her cousin Whitney Houston for "Saving All My Love for You."

Accepting the Song of the Year, reigning King of Pop Michael Jackson struck a grand note, saying, "I'd like to thank God ... for choosing [cowriter]

Left page: *Whitney Houston*
This page: *Sting*

**WINNER SNAPSHOT**
**Record of the Year**
"We Are the World" • USA for Africa (Various Artists)
**Album of the Year**
*No Jacket Required* • Phil Collins
**Song of the Year**
"We Are the World" • Michael Jackson & Lionel Richie, songwriters

**Best New Artist**
Sade
**SPECIAL MERIT AWARDS**
Lifetime Achievement Award
Benny Goodman, Rolling Stones, Andrés Segovia

Trustees Award
George Gershwin & Ira Gershwin

Lionel [Richie] and I to write 'We Are the World.'"

Barbra Streisand offered a heartfelt presentation of a posthumous Trustees Award to the legendary songwriting team of George and Ira Gershwin. "Like the love in the last song they ever wrote together, their music is definitely here to stay," Streisand noted, before Ira Gershwin's widow, Leonore, graciously accepted the award.

Ronnie Milsap's big country hit "Lost in the Fifties Tonight (In the Still of the Night)"—which would win the Grammy for Best Country Vocal Performance, Male—became the jumping off point for an ambitious '50s medley that featured Milsap, Fred Parris and The Five Satins, Carl Perkins, and Huey Lewis & The News.

A salute to the Rolling Stones began with Kenny Rogers singing their praises, saying "They set a tone for rock music for the next generation that made it okay to play from your heart ... and sometimes even lower." Then Eric Clapton appeared via satellite with the Stones

from the Roof Garden Club in London. "As far as I'm concerned, they are what rock and roll is all about—toughness and relentless to the very end," Clapton said. Slowhand then presented the band with the Lifetime Achievement Award, noting they were "the most volatile and intact rock group to survive the '60s." The band seemed to be having a very good night indeed, and Mick Jagger offered these words: "I'd like to say thank you to all the people that have stuck by this band through thick and thin. And to all the people that took the piss, the joke's on you."

The final award of the evening was Record of the Year, and in accepting for "We Are the World," producer Quincy Jones made reference to that famous "Check Your Ego at the Door" sign outside the recording sessions for the song. "It was never necessary," Jones said warmly. And then he set the stage for many more such high-minded musical efforts in the future, saying, "I hope it becomes fashionable."

*Did You Know ...?* The Best Polka Recording category is introduced. The first winner is Frank Yankovic for 70 Years of Hits. • DeLeon Richards, known as "the Young Gospel Sensation," becomes the youngest nominee, at 9 years old, for her album Deleon in the category Best Soul Gospel Performance, Female.

# 29th Annual Grammy Awards

## SHRINE AUDITORIUM, LOS ANGELES

*Eligibility Year: October 1, 1985–September 30, 1986*
*Announced on February 24, 1987*

*Paul Simon's* performance of "Diamonds on the Soles of Her Shoes" with Ladysmith Black Mambazo from the *Graceland* album opened the 29th Annual Grammy Awards on a boldly beautiful and global note, offering a soulful reaffirmation of the reach and relevance of truly great music. It also provided first-time host Billy Crystal with a devilishly funny opening line. "Is it just me," the comedian wondered aloud, "or did Art Garfunkel look different?"

Simon—still sans Garfunkel—would ultimately return to the stage when Whoopi Goldberg and Don Johnson—in matching *Miami Vice* suits—presented him with the final award of the evening, Album of the Year. In his gracious acceptance speech, Simon ended by expressing "my deep admiration and love for the singers and musicians from South Africa who worked with me on *Graceland*.... They live, along with other South African artists and their countrymen, under one of the most repressive regimes on the planet today, and still they are able to produce music of great power and

nuance and joy. And I find that just extraordinary, and they have my great respect and love."

Simon wasn't the only rock veteran winning on this Grammy night. Steve Winwood, in the midst of a major comeback, also felt some "higher love" from The Academy. The Bangles and Live Aid leader Bob Geldof presented the former Traffic leader with the first Grammy of the night for Best Pop Vocal Performance, Male. Winwood also won Record of the Year for "Higher Love," the soulful single on which he was joined by Chaka Khan. Meanwhile, the Grammy for Best Pop Vocal Performance, Female, went to Barbra Streisand for *The Broadway Album*. For Streisand, this validation represented "a reaffirmation of the stature and quality of this timeless material." She also pointed out that she had a hunch she might win since the show was on February 24, and 24 was her lucky number—she had been born on the 24th, had her son at 24, and won her first Grammy 24 years earlier. "So with your continued support and a little

**WINNER SNAPSHOT**
**Record of the Year**
"Higher Love" • Steve Winwood
**Album of the Year**
*Graceland* • Paul Simon
**Song of the Year**
"That's What Friends Are For" • Burt Bacharach & Carole Bayer Sager, songwriters
**Best New Artist**
Bruce Hornsby & The Range

bit of luck, I might just see you again 24 years from tonight."

Even by the eclectic standards of the Grammy Awards telecast, this show offered some wild stylistic shifts. Billy Idol beat out his Stax remake "To Be a Lover" in a boxing ring that could barely contain his post-punk energy. The fast-rising Beastie Boys behavior in presenting the Grammy for Best Rock Performance, Male, to Robert Palmer was such that the *New York Times*' John J. O'Connor wrote, "Among the sprinkling of younger faces, a group called the Beastie Boys did its best to be outrageous while presenting an award, but ended up looking like the Three Stooges."

But it wasn't all Beastie. One of the biggest ovations of the evening came for legendary lyric soprano Kathleen Battle and classical guitarist Christopher Parkening for a stunning rendition of "Ave Maria." The audience also gave a well-earned standing ovation for an inspired and inspiring group of R&B greats—B.B. King, Albert King, Etta James, Willie Dixon, Koko Taylor, Junior Wells, Big Jay McNealy, Dr. John, and recent sensation Robert Cray, who managed to let the good times roll during a salute to the blues that featured the backing of guitarist Ry Cooder, bassist Tim Drummond, and drummer Jim Keltner. Also impressive were three of country's bright new male stars—Steve Earle, Randy

Travis, and Dwight Yoakam—who all gave strong performances before the Best Country Vocal Solo Performance, Male, award for which they were nominated went to veteran Ronnie Milsap.

The award for Song of the Year went to Burt Bacharach and Carole Bayer Sager for "That's What Friends Are For"—which became a heartening, conscious, and inescapable fund-raising response to the AIDS crisis as recorded by the fabulous foursome of Dionne Warwick, Elton John, Gladys Knight, and Stevie Wonder (according to Sager this night, the song had raised $750,000). That recording was also recognized with the Grammy for Best Pop Performance by a Duo or Group with Vocal. And on this night, Warwick, Knight, and Wonder performed it with the accompaniment of Bacharach himself on piano.

Accepting the Song of the Year award, Bacharach seemed genuinely moved. "Of all the songs that I've written, [this is] the one song when I still hear on the radio or hear in performance, I get a little teary in my eyes and a little touched—goose bumps," Bacharach confessed. "I think it goes way beyond the song—it's a good song, I'm proud of the song. I think it goes to the outer fringe of what that song has meant to so many people—in joy, sadness, heartbreak and hope and friendship and love."

Left page clockwise from top left: Billy Idol • Janet Jackson performs "What Have You Done for Me Lately?" • Bruce Hornsby • Paul Simon with Ladysmith Black Mambazo This page: Christopher Parkening and Kathleen Battle

*Did You Know ...?* Elton John earns his first win, 16 years after his first nomination, for "That's What Friends Are For" (with Dionne Warwick, Gladys Knight, and Stevie Wonder) in Best Pop Performance by a Duo Group with Vocal. • Eurythmics receive their only Grammy, for "Missionary Man" in Best Rock Performance by a Duo or Group with Vocal. • Reba McEntire wins her first time nominated for her recording of "Whoever's in New England" in Best Country Vocal Performance, Female.

# 30th Annual Grammy Awards

RADIO CITY MUSIC HALL, NEW YORK

*Eligibility Year: October 1, 1986–September 30, 1987*
*Announced on March 2, 1988*

On March 2, 1988, the Grammy Awards returned for the first time in seven years to New York City for its 30th birthday party. "This is a historic building," host Billy Crystal explained, talking about Radio City Music Hall. "Because it's the only building Donald Trump doesn't own … *yet*."

No single star owned the night of the 30th Annual Grammy Awards show, but in terms of both awards and performances, this proved to be a very good night for many of music's elite. Take U2: The Irish rock gods won Album of the Year and Best Rock Performance by a Duo or Group with Vocal for *The Joshua Tree*. Accepting the latter award, U2 guitarist The Edge offered the most memorable run of thank-yous in Grammy history, proclaiming, "I'd like to thank Desmond Tutu for his courage, Martin Luther King, Bob Dylan for 'Tangled Up in Blue,' Flannery O'Connor, Jimi Hendrix, Walt Disney, John the Baptist, Georgie Best, Gregory Peck, James T. Kirk, Morris Pratt, Dr. Ruth, Fawn Hall, Batman and Robin, Lucky the Dog, Pee Wee Herman, the YMCA, Eddie the Eagle, sumo wrestlers throughout the world, and, of course, Ronald Reagan."

Bono—never one to be outdone in the speaking department—took a more serious tone in accepting the Grammy for Album of the Year, explaining that U2 set out to make soul music. "It's not about being black or white, or the instruments you play or whether you use a drum machine or not. It's a decision to reveal or conceal. And without it people like Prince would be nothing more than [the] brilliant song-and-dance man that he is, but he's much more than that. People like Bruce Springsteen would be nothing more than a great storyteller, but he's much more than that. Without it … U2 certainly wouldn't be here, and we are here, and I wouldn't want to be anywhere else than New York City tonight."

Left page:
*Michael Jackson*
This page: *George Strait earns his first Grammy nomination: "All My Ex's Live in Texas" in the Best Country Vocal Performance, Male, category*

**WINNER SNAPSHOT**
**Record of the Year**
"Graceland" • Paul Simon
**Album of the Year**
*The Joshua Tree* • U2
**Song of the Year**
"Somewhere Out There" • James Horner, Barry Mann &
Cynthia Weil, songwriters

**Best New Artist**
Jody Watley

New York City figured prominently in many of the night's most magical moments, including an incredible Big Apple music segment that featured wonderful turns for George Benson performing his hit cover of "On Broadway," a remarkably energetic Cab Calloway doing "Minnie the Moocher," Tito Puente and Celia Cruz ("Quimbara"), Lou Reed ("Walk on the Wild Side"), Run-D.M.C. ("Tougher Than Leather"), Michael Brecker (substituting for an ailing Miles Davis), Marcus Miller and David Sanborn ("Tutu"), and Billy Joel performing "New York State of Mind." Later, Billy Crystal revealed that he and homeboy Billy Joel had more than a first name in common. "My first paying job as a comedian was opening for Billy Joel at Fairleigh Dickinson in Teaneck, New Jersey," Crystal explained. "Now I'm here doing this show and he's a five-time Grammy winner."

Also winning was a big celebration of doo-wop— "the stuff we sang in the men's room in high school because the echo was so great," as Crystal said in the introduction. With famed New York disc jockey Jocko Henderson as the narrator, the extended, harmonic convergence included appearances by the Angels, the Cadillacs, Dion, the Flamingos, and the Regents, along with Lou Reed, Ruben Blades, and Buster Poindexter.

An even earlier rock great, Little Richard, made a brilliantly hysterical and rapturously received commotion in copresenting with Poindexter the Best New Artist award to Jody Watley. Before announcing the actual winner, Little Richard repeatedly declared himself the winner, as well as a "brown Jew from Georgia" and "the architect of rock and roll." Later, Crystal announced that Little Richard would be releasing new versions of his old hits—"Long Tall Shirley," "Good Golly Miss Molly Goldberg," and "Tutti Frutti, So Sue Me."

Somewhat less winning was the often hilarious Jackie Mason, whose stand-up performance met considerable audience resistance when he came across to many as being less than properly respectful to the rightly beloved Quincy Jones. On the other hand, Jones' collaborator Michael Jackson nearly stole the show performing "The Way You Make Me Feel" and "Man in the Mirror" with great finesse and style. Whitney Houston also made a big impression—opening the telecast with "I Wanna Dance with Somebody (Who Loves Me)," the same song that earned her the Best Pop Vocal Performance, Female, Grammy later in the evening.

All in all, the Grammy's 30th anniversary party in Radio City turned out to be something Bono would approve of—a pretty soulful night of music.

Left page clockwise from top left: *Billy Crystal • Run-D.M.C. • U2 with Brian Eno, Daniel Lanois, and presenter Herb Alpert • Tito Puente and Celia Cruz* This page: *Jody Watley and Little Richard*

*Did You Know ...? Frank Zappa and his son Dweezil Zappa are both nominated in the Best Rock Instrumental Performance (Orchestra, Group or Soloist) category, with Frank taking home the Grammy for his* Jazz from Hell *album. • "Somewhere Out There" becomes the first song from an animated film (*An American Tail*) to win Song of the Year.*

# 31st Annual Grammy Awards

SHRINE AUDITORIUM, LOS ANGELES
Eligibility Year: October 1, 1987–September 30, 1988
Announced on February 22, 1989

*Following* Whitney Houston's inspired opening performance of "One Moment in Time"—a song she recorded for the 1988 Summer Olympics in Seoul, South Korea—host Billy Crystal proclaimed, "This year promises to be a kinder, gentler Grammy," borrowing one of then-President George H.W. Bush's stated objectives for the nation.

Ultimately, it wasn't all kinder and gentler—however, it was a year in which Bobby McFerrin's famously upbeat "Don't Worry, Be Happy" was named Record of the Year, Song of the Year, and Best Pop Vocal Performance, Male, not to mention another McFerrin win for Best Jazz Vocal Performance, Male, for a different song ("Brothers"). McFerrin—billed by Crystal as "the Grammy Symphony Orchestra"—also performed a wide-ranging and witty history of music, vocalizing as Crystal spoke.

Yet this was also a very big year for Tracy Chapman, whose "Fast Car" spoke powerfully to real-life worries and the eternal desire for escape. By the end of the evening at the Shrine Auditorium in Los Angeles, Chapman was named Best New Artist and took home the Grammy Award for Best Pop Vocal Performance, Female, and Best Contemporary Folk Recording.

Other performing artists brought a welcome edge to the 31st proceedings, including the always-interesting Sinéad O'Connor performing "Mandinka" from her debut album, *The Lion and the Cobra*, and Lyle Lovett, who brought his brilliantly offbeat brand of down-home music to a country sequence that also featured a memorable duet by Dwight Yoakam and Buck Owens on "Streets of Bakersfield."

But it was the addition of some new metal at the 31st Grammy Awards that would prove more controversial. During the show, Crystal explained, "Not too long ago heavy metal was confined to the underground, but times change and the Grammys change with the times. And we

*Left page: Lyle Lovett*
*This page: Tracy Chapman*

acknowledge the art form that is keeping the rebellious essence of rock and roll alive and have added a Grammy Award in that category for the first time this year." The new category was called Best Hard Rock/Metal Performance, Vocal or Instrumental, and Crystal then introduced one of the nominees—Metallica. The group performed a characteristically intense and explosive version of "One" from the album …*And Justice for All* (which likely included the first use of machine gun sound effects on the Grammys). However, when Alice Cooper and Lita Ford came out to present the award, the Grammy went to veteran rock act Jethro Tull—a fine group of longstanding musicians, but arguably the least hard or metal of the nominees. The category and Metallica performance were proof of Grammy's ambition, though the category proved too broad. The next year it would be dubbed more purely Best Metal Performance, and Metallica would take the prize.

In an ever changing musical world, the 31st Annual Grammys also significantly marked the very first year of the Best Rap Performance category with the award going to DJ Jazzy Jeff & The Fresh Prince for "Parents Just Don't Understand" during the pre-telecast ceremonies. As presenter Kool Moe Dee eloquently commented: "On the behalf of all MCs, my coworkers, and fellow nomi-

nees—Jazzy Jeff, J.J. Fad, Salt-N-Pepa, and the boy who's bad—we personify power and a drug-free mind, and we express ourselves through rhythm and rhyme. So I think it's time that the whole world knows rap is here to stay."

Linda Ronstadt, meanwhile, showcased her Mexican-American heritage with a fine performance of "La Charreada" from her winning *Canciones De Mi Padre*, complete with a mariachi band and dancers. She followed this performance by taking home the Best Mexican-American Performance Grammy.

Other moments on this show were reminders of the Grammy Award's unique ability to blend genres and bring together generations with ease and grace. Three Lifetime Achievement Award recipients—Leontyne Price, Sarah Vaughan, and Dizzy Gillespie—all gave vital, crowd-pleasing performances, and famed violinist Itzhak Perlman made an excellent point when he noted that he was happy to see classical music doing so well in the "race for space on the Grammy show. We may not sell as many records as our associates in the pop, rock, and country fields, but you must admit our hits last a long time."

On the Grammy Awards telecast, it's all good in the end. As Billy Crystal rightly said in his closing thought for the night: "The more you love music, the more music you love."

Left page clockwise from top left: *Dizzy Gillespie • Bobby McFerrin • Sinéad O'Connor • Alice Cooper and Lita Ford* This page: *Metallica's James Hetfield*

# 1990s

The last decade of the 20th century marked the last breaths of the Cold War, the remarkable rise of the grunge movement and the hard fall of the hair band. Bill Clinton became arguably our most rock and roll president to date—and a future Grammy winner, too—while the Internet created a digital revolution with which the music industry is still reckoning. Responding—though some would argue cautiously—the Grammy Awards also continued to evolve to honor more rap and alternative rock. Still, the decade's big Grammy winners included veterans from Natalie Cole with her late great father Nat "King" Cole, Eric Clapton, Whitney Houston, Tony Bennett, and Carlos Santana to some notable, newer Grammy faces such as Sheryl Crow, Seal, Celine Dion, Alison Krauss, and Lauryn Hill. And when Nirvana finally won Best Alternative Music Performance for their *MTV Unplugged in New York* in mid-decade, it may have been too little, too late for Kurt Cobain, but it was at least a recognition that our musical teen spirit had changed dramatically.

# 32nd Annual Grammy Awards

SHRINE AUDITORIUM, LOS ANGELES
*Eligibility Year: October 1, 1988–September 30, 1989*
*Announced on February 21, 1990*

When the final award for Record of the Year was presented to "Wind Beneath My Wings," Bette Midler charmingly summed up this whole 32nd Annual Grammy night by gleefully proclaiming, "Hey, Bonnie Raitt, I got one too!"

Coming fittingly just in the nick of time, veteran rootsy singer and guitar-slinger Raitt thoroughly enjoyed an altogether satisfying Grammy night—winning Album of the Year for her *Nick of Time* comeback, along with Best Pop Vocal Performance, Female, Best Rock Vocal Performance, Female, and Best Traditional Blues Recording for a duet with John Lee Hooker ("I'm in the Mood," on Hooker's *The Healer*). Having famously bounced back from substance abuse problems and having been dropped by her former label, Raitt won her first four Grammys ever in just a matter of hours—a global media event that would subsequently help make the Don Was–produced *Nick of Time* an even bigger hit. For her part, Raitt—who performed "Thing Called Love" on the show—was increasingly shocked as her awards piled up. "This is a real miracle for me after all this time," she said.

Raitt graciously thanked her peers for nominating her in previous years "when things weren't going so well." Alluding gracefully to her past troubles, she also noted, "And mostly I'd like to thank God for bringing me to this at a time when I could truly appreciate it."

The other moving centerpiece of this first Grammy show held in the '90s—wonderfully hosted by Garry Shandling—was a suitably grand and heartfelt salute to one of the night's Lifetime Achievement Award recipients, Paul McCartney.

Speaking lovingly for her boomer generation, Meryl Streep presented the tribute, first recalling her own experience seeing the Beatles at Shea Stadium in 1965 from the 116th row with an "I Love You Forever Paul" sign in her hands. "I had a better view of New Jersey than I did of the little stage that was set up on centerfield," she said with a smile. Still, Streep beautifully recalled seeing "those four boys running across the grass to the stage" and "the roar that just rose up." Streep then introduced two of McCartney's own favorites to perform two of his songs. Ray Charles served up the funkiest version ever of "Eleanor

*Left page: Bonnie Raitt*
*This page: Bette Midler*

**WINNER SNAPSHOT**
**Record of the Year**
"Wind Beneath My Wings" • Bette Midler
**Album of the Year**
*Nick of Time* • Bonnie Raitt
**Song of the Year**
"Wind Beneath My Wings" • Larry Henley & Jeff Silbar, songwriters

**SPECIAL MERIT AWARDS**
Lifetime Achievement Award
Nat "King" Cole, Miles Davis,
Vladimir Horowitz, Paul McCartney

Trustees Award
Dick Clark

Legend Award
Liza Minnelli, Willie Nelson, Smokey Robinson,
Andrew Lloyd Webber

Rigby," while Stevie Wonder offered up a believably optimistic version of "We Can Work It Out."

Following one of the more extended standing ovations in all of Grammy history, McCartney took the stage and kissed Streep, adding, "Thank you, Meryl, I remember you well—row 116." McCartney then spoke eloquently of his love for the music of Charles and Wonder, of environmental challenges the world faced, of his family, and of his pleasure in joining "the best band in the world—thanks John, George, and Ringo for being beautiful people." McCartney concluded memorably, "I'd like to thank you all for being in my dream."

Yet on an evening where the sublime dominated splendidly, there was one unfortunate yet notable touch of the ridiculous when soon-to-be-exposed lip-synchers Milli Vanilli were presented with the Grammy for Best New Artist. The award was officially withdrawn later in 1990 when it was confirmed by producer Frank Farian that on the supposed duo's debut album *All or Nothing*, "front men" Fab Morvan and Rob Pilatus had actually sang not all but *nothing*. The pair did, however, dance energetically and manage to at least partially mouth the lyrics to their smash "Girl You Know It's True" during the show. (Commenting on the performance, Shandling explained, "I was supposed to be in that number. I wouldn't wear the extensions.")

The 32nd Annual Grammy Awards was also historic for featuring the first-ever televised rap award (the category had been established the year prior). First, during a

performance of "I Think I Can Beat Mike Tyson" by DJ Jazzy Jeff & the Fresh Prince, Will Smith dedicated the group's performance "to all the rappers last year that stood with us and helped us to earn the right to be on this stage tonight." Then teen dreams New Kids on the Block presented the award, with the group's Donnie Wahlberg respectfully name-checking hip-hop pioneers Afrika Bambaataa, Grandmaster Flash, Grandmaster Melle Mel, Run-D.M.C., and Kurtis Blow, before handing out the award for Best Rap Performance to Young MC for "Bust a Move." Adding a little hip-hop edge to the proceedings, Public Enemy's Flavor Flav proceeded to join Young MC onstage uninvited. "I'd like to thank Flavor Flav for breaking up the monotony of my acceptance speech," Young MC noted.

The night featured many other musical highlights, including a performance by Lifetime Achievement recipient Miles Davis, a short impromptu version of "Straighten Up and Fly Right" by Ella Fitzgerald and Natalie Cole on a night when the late Nat "King" Cole was also honored with a Lifetime Achievement Award, and a haunting rendition of "Summertime" from *Porgy and Bess* by Metropolitan Opera star Harolyn Blackwell.

The 32nd Annual Grammys also included perhaps the single finest dirty joke inspired by a format change in all of music history. As Shandling memorably explained, "Compact discs are overtaking the business, of course, which is ruining my life because I make love to music and I *cannot* find 45s anymore."

Left page clockwise from top left: *DJ Jazzy Jeff & the Fresh Prince • Don Henley • Milli Vanilli • Michael Bolton and Kenny G*
This page: *Paul McCartney*

*Did You Know ...?* Hank Williams Jr. and his father Hank Williams Sr. win for their recording "There's a Tear in My Beer" in Best Country Vocal Collaboration. • Johnny Cash and his daughter Rosanne Cash are nominated for separate recordings—Johnny for "Will the Circle Be Unbroken" (with other artists) in Best Country Vocal Collaboration and Rosanne for "I Don't Want to Spoil the Party" in Best Country Vocal Performance, Female. • A special "Grammy Legends" show honoring Liza Minnelli, Willie Nelson, Smokey Robinson, and Andrew Lloyd Webber airs in November 1989.

# 33rd Annual Grammy Awards

RADIO CITY MUSIC HALL, NEW YORK

*Eligibility Year: October 1, 1989–September 30, 1990*
*Announced on February 20, 1991*

The grunge revolution was just about to hit the music world, but the 33rd Annual Grammy Awards were about more than just teen spirit. Quincy Jones took home the Album of the Year for his blockbuster *Back on the Block* album, while Roy Orbison posthumously won the Grammy for Best Pop Vocal Performance, Male, for a re-recording of his classic "Oh, Pretty Woman." At the same time, younger artists had breakout years, including Mariah Carey, who won the Best New Artist Grammy as well as Best Pop Vocal Performance, Female ("Vision of Love"), and Living Colour, who took home the Grammy for Best Hard Rock Performance ("Time's Up").

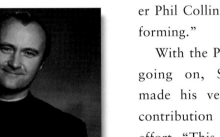

Then there's the man who had 10 nominations for the night, ultimately winning one big award for Record of the Year: Phil Collins for "Another Day in Paradise." It was a good thing that the former Genesis drummer won one as he was becoming a Grammy fixture. In his opening monologue at Radio City Music Hall, host Garry Shandling dryly explained, "If you at home want to know, by the way, how they decide each year where to hold the Grammys, it's simply wherever Phil Collins is already performing."

With the Persian Gulf War going on, Shandling then made his very own special contribution to the wartime effort. "This is going tonight … to our troops in the Middle East," the host told the audience. "Fellas, we'll try to get as many tight shots of Chynna Phillips and Mariah Carey as we can, alright? And for you women in the Gulf, of course, we have Richard Gere and myself you can look at."

Richard Gere was indeed in attendance to emcee the Lifetime Achievement Award tribute that included Tracy Chapman playing "Imagine" at the piano and Aerosmith rocking up "Come Together" to honor John Lennon. Gere explained that Lennon

**WINNER SNAPSHOT**
**Record of the Year**
"Another Day in Paradise" • Phil Collins
**Album of the Year**
*Back on the Block* • Quincy Jones
**Song of the Year**
"From a Distance" • Julie Gold, songwriter
**Best New Artist**
Mariah Carey

**SPECIAL MERIT AWARDS**
Lifetime Achievement Award
Marian Anderson, Bob Dylan,
John Lennon, Kitty Wells

Trustees Award
Milt Gabler, Berry Gordy,
Sam Phillips
Legend Award
Johnny Cash, Aretha Franklin, Billy Joel, Quincy Jones

was being honored "for redefining the subject matter and musical content of popular music and for his extraordinary ability as a musician, singer, songwriter, philosopher, communicator, and activist for peace, love, and understanding and might I say total nonviolence." Yoko Ono accepted the award and spoke to the moment. "Pray for the safety and health of this beautiful planet," she said. "John Lennon would have liked that." In accepting the Song of the Year Grammy for the spiritually minded "From a Distance" —which Bette Midler made a smash—songwriter Julie Gold made another memorable plea: "To the soldiers everywhere, we pray for your speedy return. We pray for peace on earth."

You might have thought that Quincy Jones would have been used to winning Grammy Awards, but winning Album of the Year clearly meant a lot to him. "I've been in this Academy since 1958 and this is the first time I even dared thinking about having a Grammy under my own name, and I'm so proud." Jones went on to mention the age difference between himself and one of the members of Wilson Phillips, nominated in the same category along with albums by Phil Collins, Mariah Carey, and MC Hammer. "When Chynna

Phillips was about six months old, Jack Nicholson used to bring her around the house, and now we're in the same category," he said with a smile. "I was about to retire." Jones had a great night overall. In addition to Album of the Year, he took home Grammys for Best Arrangement on an Instrumental and Best Jazz Fusion Performance ("Birdland"), Best Instrumental Arrangement Accompanying Vocal ("The Places You Find Love"), Best Rap Performance by a Duo or Group ("Back on the Block"), and Producer of the Year, Non-Classical.

The most eloquent words of the night actually came from Nicholson, who introduced Bob Dylan's performance of "Masters of War" and presented him with his Lifetime Achievement Award. Of the man he lovingly called "Uncle Bobby," Nicholson said this: "He's been called everything from the voice of his generation to the conscience of the world. He rejects both titles and any others that try to categorize him or analyze him. He opened the doors of pop music wider than anybody else, yet returned time and again to the simplicity of basic chords and emotions to express himself. He's been and still is a disturber of the peace—his own as well as ours."

Left page clockwise from top left: *Living Colour* • *MC Hammer* • *Harry Connick Jr. receives the Best Jazz Vocal Performance, Male, Grammy from Quincy Jones* This page: *Jack Nicholson and Bob Dylan*

*Did You Know …?* Sinéad O'Connor wins the first ever Best Alternative Music Performance Grammy for I Do Not Want What I Haven't Got. • Comedian/actor George Burns, the oldest winner ever at the age of 95, wins Best Spoken Word or Non-Musical Recording for Gracie: A Love Story. • Ella Fitzgerald enjoys her final nomination and win for "All That Jazz" in the Best Jazz Vocal Performance category. Throughout her career she would receive 20 nominations and 13 wins.

# 34th Annual Grammy Awards

RADIO CITY MUSIC HALL, NEW YORK

*Eligibility Year: October 1, 1990–September 30, 1991*
*Announced on February 25, 1992*

*Unforgettable* — that's what the 34th Annual Grammy Awards show at Radio City Music Hall in New York was. Natalie Cole's salute to the music of her legendary father Nat "King" Cole was remembered with many awards—winning Record of the Year, Album of the Year, Song of the Year, Best Traditional Pop Performance, Best Instrumental Arrangement Accompanying Vocals, Best Engineered Album, Non-Classical—while her producer David Foster took home the Grammy for Producer of the Year (Non-Classical). Accepting the Song of the Year Grammy for "Unforgettable," veteran songwriter Irving Gordon described the experience nicely. "It's like being caught in the middle of a miracle," he explained. "In a youth-oriented culture—where youth is worshipped—it's nice to have a middle-aged song do something."

All ages were represented on the show, hosted by Whoopi Goldberg. As Johnny Mathis said to his copresenter Dionne Warwick, "I just love the Grammys. On what other list would I find my name between Madonna and Megadeth?"

Paul Simon got things off to an impressively rhythmic start with an opening performance of "Cool, Cool River" from his *Rhythm of the Saints* album. A dreadlocked Seal made a memorable live American debut performing his first smash "Crazy." Michael Bolton sang his hit version of "When a Man Loves a Woman" and won the Grammy for Best Pop Vocal Performance, Male. And Mary Chapin Carpenter added a bit of Cajun spice to the proceedings by performing "Down at the Twist and Shout" with the great rootsy band BeauSoleil. After being presented with the Grammy for Best Country Vocal Performance, Female, by Clint Black and the legendary Roy Rogers, Carpenter thanked the group for "injecting such magic and joy" into "Down at the Twist and Shout."

*Left page: LL Cool J performs "Mama Said Knock You Out," which wins Best Rap Solo Performance*
*This page: Natalie Cole*

Host Goldberg added a different sort of spice and comic relief—even making perhaps the dirtiest sounding joke in Grammy history about the show accountants. "I must tell you Deloitte & Touche are two things I do nightly," she said, before reporting that the accountants would be heading out on tour with Guns N' Roses.

Not everybody was joking around. When R.E.M. won the Grammy for Best Pop Performance by a Duo or Group with Vocal ("Losing My Religion") —one of their three awards for the night—singer Michael Stipe struck a progressive political note. "We'd like to urge everybody to register and vote in the United States," Stipe said of the looming 1992 presidential election that would eventually bring Bill Clinton into his first term in office. "We need candidates who will really address important issues—homelessness, AIDS research, economic depression, and national healthcare." He said this while wearing a hat with the words "White House Stop AIDS."

Academy President Michael Greene spoke about the government's America 2000 plan, the Bush Administration's educational strategy of nationwide goals in the new millennium, pointing out, "Among

all the goals, the words 'art' or 'music' are not mentioned even one time. The very idea that you can educate young people in a meaningful way without music and art is simply absurd." Then, after recognizing Muddy Waters, John Coltrane, Jimi Hendrix, and James Brown with Lifetime Achievement Awards, Greene honored Academy Executive Vice President Christine Farnon with the Trustees Award. In paying tribute to Farnon's 30-plus years of service, he said, "From its earliest days when The Recording Academy was little more than a dream, a letterhead and a golden statue of an antique phonograph, [The Recording Academy] was nurtured and protected by a caring, deeply dedicated professional."

Stephen Sondheim appeared to honor one of the greatest female stars of the century. "She's as good as they come," Sondheim told the Radio City Music Hall audience. "Tonight she is a Grammy legend. Her name is Barbra Streisand." He went on to present her with the Grammy Legend Award for "her relentless pursuit of perfection." For her part, Streisand struck a humble note: "In all honesty, I don't feel like a legend. I feel more like a work in progress."

Left page clockwise from top left: *Barbra Streisand* • *R.E.M.* • *Seal* • *Clint Black and Roy Rogers* • *Amy Grant* • *Bonnie Raitt accepts one of her three Grammy wins*
This page: *Vince Gill*

*Did You Know ...?* In accepting Metallica's award for Best Metal Performance with Vocal for Metallica, *Lars Ulrich jokes, "Thanks to Jethro Tull for not putting out an album this year," a nod to both Tull's surprise win over Metallica in the metal category's first year and to Paul Simon's much earlier, similar reference to multiple Album of the Year winner Stevie Wonder.* • *The Grammys add a Best World Music Album category among several others. Grateful Dead drummer Mickey Hart's* Planet Drum *wins.*

# 35th Annual Grammy Awards

*In the midst* of the 35th Annual Grammy Awards, host Garry Shandling considered the way things were going and told the star-studded audience at the Shrine Auditorium in Los Angeles, "Okay, I'll go out on a limb and say if you're up against Eric Clapton in any other categories, I'd go home now. It's a feeling I have."

Shandling's hunch would prove to be a very solid one. In recognition of Clapton's deeply moving song "Tears in Heaven"—inspired by the death of his 4-year-old son Conor—and for his successful *Unplugged* album, he received a grand total of six Grammy Awards: Record of the Year, Album of the Year, Song of the Year, Best Pop Vocal Performance, Male, Best Rock Vocal Performance, Male, and Best Rock Song. Throughout the night, Clapton seemed surprised by the outpouring and remained

rather low-key. But when he won the night's final award for Record of the Year, Clapton plainly but powerfully explained, "The one person I want to thank is my son for the love he gave me and the song he gave me."

Clearly, this was an emotional night for the veteran rock guitar god, and rock stars of a certain age seemed to be on Shandling's mind as well right from the start. Referencing the recent election of President Bill Clinton, Shandling noted, "My generation's becoming the mainstream here. It's very weird. Mick Jagger is older than the president of the United States. It's a very spooky time." Shandling also offered a brilliant bit of stand-up comedy/political commentary about Clinton, referencing the president's famous campaign sound bite regarding whether or not he smoked

Left page: *Anthony Kiedis with George Clinton*
This page: *Eric Clapton*

pot: "He plays the sax. He plays it, sort of. He plays like a guy who never inhaled, but hey …"

Ultimately, though, the spirit of the Grammys is nothing if not multigenerational and the night's other big winners included the upstart hip-hop group Arrested Development, who took home not only the Best New Artist award, but also the Grammy for Best Rap Performance by a Duo or a Group ("Tennessee"). A still up-and-coming Celine Dion won the Best Pop Performance by a Duo or Group with Vocal along with

Peabo Bryson for "Beauty and the Beast" from the Disney film of the same name (the soundtrack album would help generate five awards on this night). The Grammy for Best Hard Rock Performance with Vocal went to the Red Hot Chili Peppers, who provided the Grammy show with perhaps its most freewheeling highlight—a version of "Give It Away" that found a creatively attired Peppers joined by their longtime influence and onetime producer George Clinton along with his P-Funk All-Stars. Another memorable performance was Peter Gabriel's telecast-opening version of "Steam" that featured Cirque du Soleil; Gabriel won Best Music Video, Short Form, for "Digging

in the Dirt." Another altogether jazzy standout performance came from Arturo Sandoval and the GRP All-Stars who served up a searing version of "Cherokee."

Even without performing, Michael Jackson provided a significant amount of the evening's entertainment. First, Jackson's recent highly rated 90-minute prime-time interview with Oprah Winfrey provided Shandling with one of his biggest laughs. "To insure higher ratings this year on the Grammys, I will be interviewing him the last 90 minutes of the show. And I'll be asking him hard-hitting questions, too, things like, 'Hey Michael, [can I] get you anything?'"

Remarkably, Jackson may have actually topped Shandling when he accepted his Grammy Legend Award from his sister Janet Jackson. Before launching into a fascinating speech about his childhood being stolen from him, Jackson pulled off a completely surprising punch line. "I hope this finally puts to rest another rumor that's been in the press for too many years," Jackson said, standing next to his chart-topping sibling. "Me and Janet really are two different people."

*Did You Know …? Earvin "Magic" Johnson (with Robert O'Keefe) wins in the Best Spoken Word or Non-Musical Album for* What You Can Do To Avoid AIDS.

# 36th Annual Grammy Awards

RADIO CITY MUSIC HALL, NEW YORK

*Eligibility Year: October 1, 1992–September 30, 1993*
*Announced on March 1, 1994*

Whitney Houston was already a star for many years by the time of the 36th Annual Grammy Awards, winning her first Grammy eight years earlier. Yet it was this night that represented a stunning high point in Houston's career. The singer and newly popular actress opened the show with a breathtakingly glamorous and suitably movie star–like performance of "I Will Always Love You"—the Dolly Parton classic Houston made her own on *The Bodyguard* soundtrack. Throughout the night, the audience would get to see a lot more of Houston—in the end, she won the awards for Record of the Year, Album of the Year, and Best Pop Vocal Performance, Female, while her producer David Foster took home the award for Producer of the Year.

There were other notable winners at the 36th Annual Grammy Awards show, including Toni Braxton, who won Best New Artist and actually triumphed over Houston in the Best R&B Vocal Performance, Female, category ("Another Sad Love Song"). It was also an extremely animated evening for composer Alan Menken, who won four awards for music connected to the animated movie smash *Aladdin*: Song of the Year for "A Whole New World" (sung by Regina Belle and Peabo Bryson), which Menken wrote with Tim Rice; Best Musical Album for Children; Best Instrumental Composition for a Motion Picture or for Television; and Best Song Written Specifically for a Motion Picture or for Television.

But it was the fascinating mutual admiration society of U2's Bono and Frank Sinatra that created a good deal of buzz regarding this Grammy night. First, Bono surprised many by dropping the "F-bomb" into his solo acceptance speech for the Best Alternative Music Album award for *Zooropa*. Perhaps surprised to have won the award over such nominees as Nirvana, R.E.M., and the Smashing Pumpkins, Bono proclaimed, "I think I'd like to give a message to the young people of America—and that is we shall continue to abuse our position and fuck up the mainstream. God bless you."

Left page: *Whitney Houston*
This page: *Toni Braxton*

**WINNER SNAPSHOT**
**Record of the Year**
"I Will Always Love You" • Whitney Houston
**Album of the Year**
*The Bodyguard—Original Soundtrack Album* • Whitney Houston
**Song of the Year**
"A Whole New World" *(Aladdin's Theme)* • Alan Menken & Tim Rice, songwriters
**Best New Artist**
Toni Braxton

**SPECIAL MERIT AWARDS**
Lifetime Achievement Award
Bill Evans, Aretha Franklin, Artur Rubinstein

Trustees Award
Norman Granz

Technical Grammy Award
Thomas G. Stockham Jr.

Legend Award
Curtis Mayfield, Frank Sinatra

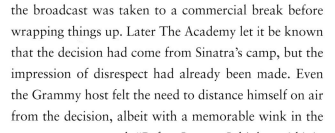

Later, Bono would strike a different tone in presenting Frank Sinatra with his Grammy Legend Award. Bono began his brilliant tone poem salute like this: "Frank never did like rock and roll. He's not crazy about guys wearing earrings either, but he doesn't hold it against me and, anyway, the feeling is not mutual. Rock and roll people love Frank Sinatra because Frank Sinatra's got what we want: swagger and attitude. He's big on attitude, serious attitude, bad attitude. Frank's Chairman of the Bad. Rock and roll plays at being tough, but this guy, well, he's the Boss. The Boss of Bosses. The Man. The Big Bang of Pop. I'm not gonna mess with him, are you?"

Sinatra's own comments would prove significantly more controversial. Sinatra—now approaching the age of 80—was clearly moved by the huge standing ovation that he received—a reaction that seemed in the moment like a massive expression of respect and multigenerational reckoning. "Thank you very much," he said, when he finally spoke. "That's the best welcome I ever had." Sinatra's comments from then on were a fascinating mix of vintage Rat Pack jokes ("This is more applause than Dean heard in his whole career"), personal thanks to his wife Barbara, and even hurt feelings that he was not asked to sing on this night. Yet, for the record, even the aging Chairman's rambling revealed singular phrasing.

Controversy ensued when Sinatra was cut off and

the broadcast was taken to a commercial break before wrapping things up. Later The Academy let it be known that the decision had come from Sinatra's camp, but the impression of disrespect had already been made. Even the Grammy host felt the need to distance himself on air from the decision, albeit with a memorable wink in the end. "Before I go on, I think you'd join me going on record that Mr. Sinatra should have finished his speech," Garry Shandling told the audience. "I think that was a slight mistake. This is live television, and I'm sure Mr. Sinatra will get even by cutting this show off in another hour."

Sinatra wasn't the only legend honored this night. Danny Glover set the stage before Lifetime Achievement Award honoree Aretha Franklin performed "(You Make Me Feel Like) A Natural Woman," noting that "There's been a 27-year love affair going on between the Grammy voters and the Queen of Soul …, [which] has produced offspring in the shape of Grammys numbering 15 so far." Upon receiving her award, Franklin proclaimed, "I'm happy. I'm honored. I'm humbled."

One of the true kings of soul—Curtis Mayfield—was also honored by a suitably soulful medley of his hits performed by Bruce Springsteen, Bonnie Raitt, B.B. King, Steve Winwood, Vernon Reid, Steve Cropper, Narada Michael Walden, and Tony! Toni! Toné! before receiving a richly deserved Grammy Legend Award, followed by an altogether fitting version of "Amen."

Left page clockwise from top: *Itzhak Perlman* • *Bono and Frank Sinatra* • *Digable Planets* This page: *Selena*

# 37th Annual Grammy Awards

*The 37th* Annual Grammy Awards struck a powerful and somber first note with Bruce Springsteen offering a no-frills performance of "Streets of Philadelphia" that was true to the drama of the song itself. Written for Jonathan Demme's film *Philadelphia*, the song was a sensitive and moving statement about the ravages of AIDS. By the end of this night, "Streets of Philadelphia" would be named Song of the Year, Best Rock Song, Best Male Rock Vocal Performance, and Best Song Written Specifically for a Motion Picture or for Television.

Springsteen handled his big night with characteristic grace and charm. "I'd like to thank all those disparaged and mysterious Grammy voters out there, wherever you are and whoever you are," he said, as he accepted the Song of the Year award from George Michael and Annie Lennox, who was wearing Mickey Mouse ears. The Boss also expressed his appreciation to "the folks who've come up to me in restaurants and on the street who've lost their sons or their lovers or their friends to AIDS and said the song meant something to them." Indeed, there were many AIDS-awareness red ribbons to be seen on the Grammys this year.

Yet on this night there was also considerable levity and, lest we forget, much music. Host Paul Reiser pointed out, "We're here to celebrate. We never go the other way. We never penalize. We never find somebody who took a good song and ruined it and drag him onstage to yell at him."

*Left page:*
*Bruce Springsteen*
*This page:*
*Melissa Etheridge*

Among those with particular reason to celebrate the 37th Annual Grammy Awards were Sheryl Crow who took home not just the Grammy Award for Best New Artist, but also Record of the Year and Best Female Pop Vocal Performance for "All I Wanna Do." Other important new voices were also recognized. After Henry Rollins successfully performed punk in a tuxedo, Soundgarden won Best Metal Performance for "Spoonman." Women dominated the rap field, with Queen Latifah taking home the Best Rap Solo Performance award for "U.N.I.T.Y.," and Salt-N-Pepa presented with the Best Rap Performance by a Duo or a Group following a standout performance of "Whatta Man" and "None of Your Business." Future Grammy favorites Green Day received the Best Alternative Rock Performance award for their breakthrough album *Dookie*.

But in the end, the big Album of the Year award went to one of the longest-standing and classiest acts in popular music history—Tony Bennett for his *MTV Unplugged* album. Bennett

seemed utterly thrilled with the recognition. "I don't believe this," said the excited vocal great. "This is the greatest moment in my whole musical career and the greatest moment [of] my whole life. There are no words. It's such a victorious feeling to sing good American music and have this happen."

Recording Academy President Michael Greene made a particularly impassioned state of the arts speech. "We are here tonight on the brink of becoming the only industrialized nation in the world with absolutely no federal support for the arts," Greene said, sounding a warning. "We must not allow the arts to be politicized, privatized, commercialized, sanitized, neutralized, or zeroed out."

Among the others honored on this night was the man who brought the Grammys to live television and television to the Grammys—Executive Producer Pierre Cossette, recognized for a quarter-century of dedicated service. Cossette's comments were brief. "My biggest job on this show every year is to keep it moving," he said, letting his Grammy team do just that.

Left page clockwise from top left: *Soundgarden • Henry Rollins • Sheryl Crow accepts Record of the Year Grammy from Anita Baker • Boyz II Men • Salt-N-Pepa* This page: *Annie Lennox*

*Did You Know ...?* In addition to receiving a Lifetime Achievement Award this year, Curtis Mayfield presented an award from his wheelchair, having been paralyzed in 1990 when a lighting rig fell on him during a concert. • Elton John wins his first Grammy as a solo performing artist for "Can You Feel the Love Tonight" in Best Male Pop Vocal Performance. • The Rolling Stones have their first and only wins this year for Voodoo Lounge *in Best Rock Album category and* "Love Is Strong" *in Best Music Video, Short Form category.*

# 38th Annual Grammy Awards

## SHRINE AUDITORIUM, LOS ANGELES

### Eligibility Year: October 1, 1994–September 30, 1995
### Announced on February 28, 1996

"This is not your father's Grammys," host Ellen DeGeneres told the crowd at the Shrine Auditorium in Los Angeles during the 38th Annual Grammy Awards. How could it be, with Alanis Morissette taking home Grammy Awards for Album of the Year and Best Rock Album for *Jagged Little Pill*, as well as Best Female Rock Vocal Performance and Best Rock Song for "You Oughta Know"—a song that could make some fathers blush?

Considerably less blush-inducing were Hootie & the Blowfish who won Best New Artist and

Best Pop Performance by a Duo or Group for "Let Her Cry." Elsewhere, Grammy winners ranged from distinguished musical veterans including Frank Sinatra (who won Best Traditional Pop Vocal Performance for *Duets II*, his first win in Grammy competition since the 9th Annual Grammy Awards in 1966) to edgier acts like Nine Inch Nails

(Best Metal Performance for "Happiness in Slavery" from *Woodstock 94*) and Nirvana (Best Alternative Music Performance for *MTV Unplugged in New York*).

This would prove to be an especially interesting night for acceptance speeches as well. Morissette went out of her way in repeated appearances to make clear that she did not feel winning the awards meant she was better than the other nominees, but rather the awards were an acknowledgement of the connection her music had made with so many listeners. However, the unofficial award for most ambivalent Grammy acceptance speech of the year had to go to Pearl Jam's Eddie Vedder when the band won Best Hard Rock Performance for "Spin the Black Circle." As Vedder said, "I just wanted to watch the show. I don't know what this means. I don't think it means anything. That's just how

*Left page: Alanis Morissette*
*This page: Ellen DeGeneres and TLC*

**WINNER SNAPSHOT**
**Record of the Year**
"Kiss from a Rose" • Seal
**Album of the Year**
*Jagged Little Pill* • Alanis Morissette
**Song of the Year**
"Kiss from a Rose" • Seal, songwriter
**Best New Artist**
Hootie & The Blowfish

173

I feel ... you've heard it all before. My dad would have liked it, but my dad died before I got to know him ... Thanks, I guess ..."

Yet it was still another acceptance that was most memorable on this evening. When Joni Mitchell's *Turbulent Indigo* was named Best Pop Album, the singer/songwriter seemed genuinely surprised and remarked that she and her co-producer and onetime husband Larry Klein "made [the] album in the state of divorcing." Klein, for his part, struck a warm and witty note when he added, "I'd like to thank Joan who is, I think, the best songwriter around these days, and thank her for 10 years of instruction." Klein then quickly added, "... in the art," lest there be any confusion about Mitchell's lessons.

Of course, there was no shortage of great musical art on display here, including three Lifetime Achievement Award recipient tributes: honoree Dave Brubeck performing a gorgeous rendition of "Blue Rondo A La Turk" with the help of newer jazz greats Roy Hargrove on trumpet and Joshua Redman on saxophone; a stunningly soulful salute to Stevie Wonder by D'Angelo and Tony Rich on dueling keyboards; and a unique pairing of soulful Brits Annie Lennox and Seal (the latter won Record and Song of the Year as well as Best Male Pop Vocal Performance for "Kiss from a Rose") to honor Marvin Gaye. The night also offered a more subdued version of "You Oughta Know" by Morissette with her band and a string section, and Mariah Carey and Boyz II Men's opening gospel-tinged rendition of "One Sweet Day." Even more uplifting was a gospel segment introduced by and featuring Whitney Houston, along with CeCe Winans and gospel great Shirley Caesar, who together brought the assembled Grammy congregation to its feet.

There was much talk on this Grammy night about recent cuts in music programs in schools, highlighted by Richard Dreyfuss, star of *Mr. Holland's Opus*, a recent movie that touched upon the importance of music education. Bobby McFerrin also spoke powerfully to this problem, telling teachers to grab a boom box and expose young minds to music by all means necessary. "Don't wait for some kind of grant to fall from the sky," he explained with the sort of clear passion for music that Grammy night has come to define.

Left page clockwise from top: *Mariah Carey and Boyz II Men* • *Coolio* • *Tupac Shakur with Kiss* • *Pearl Jam* This page: *Hootie & The Blowfish*

# 39th Annual Grammy Awards

MADISON SQUARE GARDEN, NEW YORK

*Eligibility Year: October 1, 1995–September 30, 1996*
*Announced on February 26, 1997*

*Just shy* of its 40th anniversary, the 39th Annual Grammy Awards proved to be a show for young and old—onstage and off. Fourteen-year-old country music sensation LeAnn Rimes became the youngest Grammy winner ever when Sheryl Crow, Steve Winwood, and Jakob Dylan presented her with the Best New Artist award. Later in the evening, Clint Black appeared to present an award with Rimes and confessed his own feelings of inadequacy. "When I was 14, I had a paper route," Black explained with a grin. On the other hand, this was the same night that living folk legend Pete Seeger took home the Best Traditional Folk Album at the age of 77 for *Pete*.

Marking considerable growth for the Grammys, the 39th awards achieved big firsts—playing New York's famed Madison Square Garden and moving from an auditorium to a major arena. In addition to a wide range of professional performances, this big Garden party featured a few notable appearances from nonprofessional musicians. Ellen DeGeneres—returning as Grammy host for the second year in a row—kicked things off with a song that could only be called "This Is Ellen's Grammy Song" and was backed by an all-star, all-female band that featured Bonnie Raitt, Me'Shell NdegéOcello, Shawn Colvin, Chaka Khan, and Sheila E. Even earlier in the evening—during the pretelecast awards—First Lady Hillary Rodham Clinton won a Grammy for Best Spoken Word or Non-Musical Album for the audio version of her book *It Takes a Village*. "I'm amazed," the future New York senator told the crowd. "I didn't even know that Grammys were given to tone-deaf singers like me, but I'm very grateful for this."

Fellow guitar heroes and recent collaborators Eric Clapton and Kenneth "Babyface" Edmonds teamed up for a stunning version of "Change the World" from the *Phenomenon* film soundtrack just before Bonnie

**WINNER SNAPSHOT**
**Record of the Year**
"Change the World" • Eric Clapton
**Album of the Year**
*Falling Into You* • Celine Dion
**Song of the Year**
"Change the World" • Gordon Kennedy, Wayne Kirkpatrick & Tommy Sims, songwriters
**Best New Artist**
LeAnn Rimes

**SPECIAL MERIT AWARDS**
Lifetime Achievement Award
Bobby "Blue" Bland, Everly Brothers, Judy Garland, Stéphane Grappelli, Buddy Holly, Charles Mingus, Oscar Peterson, Frank Zappa

Trustees Award
Herb Alpert & Jerry Moss, Burt Bacharach & Hal David

Technical Grammy Award
Rupert Neve

Raitt and Seal presented Clapton with the Grammy Award for Best Male Pop Vocal Performance. In his acceptance speech, Clapton took time out to praise his own favorite record of the year, Curtis Mayfield's *New World Order*. The man they call Slowhand would get more chances to speak his mind, as "Change the World" won Record of the Year as well as Song of the Year for writers Gordon Kennedy, Wayne Kirkpatrick, and Tommy Sims. Edmonds—who produced "Change the World"—was honored as Producer of the Year.

Pete Seeger—who won his award during the pretelecast—reappeared during the telecast to introduce Bruce Springsteen, who then performed "The Ghost of Tom Joad," the timely and powerful title track of the album that earned the Boss the Grammy for Best Contemporary Folk Album. For country music, too, this was also a big night in the Big Apple. Vince Gill (a two-time winner for the evening with Best Male Country Vocal Performance for "Worlds Apart" and Best Country Collaboration with Vocals for "High Lonesome Sound") led a lovely, down-home yet high-tech multiple-stage tribute to bluegrass great Bill Monroe that featured Alison Krauss and Union Station (who shared the Best Country Collaboration Grammy with Gill) and Patty Loveless.

The Fugees, meanwhile, won two awards and offered a winning take on Bob Marley's "No Woman, No Cry" with the help of Ziggy Marley, the Wailers, and the I-Threes. A tribute to jazz vocal great Ella Fitzgerald—who died on June 15, 1996—found jazz giants Herbie Hancock, Wayne Shorter, Jack DeJohnette, and Bunny Brunel backing up Natalie Cole for a rendition of "You'll Have to Swing It (Mr. Paganini)." Before she sang, Cole—the daughter of the late great Nat "King" Cole—recalled that as a child she had met Fitzgerald and Louis Armstrong. Of Lady Ella, Cole said, "She wasn't just the greatest jazz singer ever, she was the best singer I ever knew."

Beck, Toni Braxton, and Sheryl Crow were among those picking up multiple awards for the year. And this was also a fabulous Grammy night for the Beatles, who won Best Pop Performance by a Duo or Group with Vocal for their special "reunion" track "Free as a Bird" from *Anthology 1*. Director Joe Pytka's video for "Free as a Bird" also won for Best Music Video, Short Form, while the *Anthology* itself won the honors for Best Music Video, Long Form. Not bad for a band that won their last Grammy not yesterday, but nearly 30 years prior.

Left page clockwise from top left: *Rage Against the Machine wins Best Metal Performance for "Tire Me"* • *Brandy* • *Ziggy Marley with the Fugees* This page: *Beck*

*Did You Know ...?* Kenny "Babyface" Edmonds receives 12 nominations and gets three wins. • Cissy Houston has a nomination and win for Face to Face in Best Traditional Soul Gospel Album, and her daughter Whitney Houston receives three nominations, including for "Exhale (Shoop Shoop)" in Best Female R&B Vocal Performance.

# 40th Annual Grammy Awards

## RADIO CITY MUSIC HALL, NEW YORK CITY

*Eligibility Year: October 1, 1996–September 30, 1997*
*Announced on February 25, 1998*

*The Grammys* threw itself a pretty wild 40th birthday party at New York's Radio City Music Hall—a night of great highs and even some interesting lows. This was the evening that a resurgent Bob Dylan gave arguably his greatest televised performance ever with a focused and mysterious version of "Love Sick" from the Album of the Year–winning *Time Out of Mind*—only to find himself joined by an unwelcome stage crasher with the curious words "Soy Bomb" scrawled on his torso. The latter was not alone in rushing the stage—rapper Ol' Dirty Bastard of Wu-Tang Clan fame decided to take the stage during

Shawn Colvin's acceptance speech for Song of the Year ("Sunny Came Home") to declare, among other things, "Wu-Tang are for the children." Somehow it all added up to an entertaining night of surprises—pleasant or otherwise.

Hosting in a tuxedo with tails, *Frasier* star Kelsey Grammer formally addressed the matter right up front:

"The Grammys turn 40 tonight and who better to guide her into middle age than a mature, sober individual such as myself. And given the fact that four out of five of you will not get Grammys tonight, it didn't seem like a bad idea to have a psychiatrist on hand." Right he turned out to be.

It was a particularly big night for Will Smith, who opened the evening Big Willie Style performing both "Men in Black" and "Gettin' Jiggy Wit It." Even more moving was his acceptance speech for Best Rap Solo Performance. "This is actually the first time that I've ever been on a Grammy stage," Smith said, explaining that as part of DJ Jazzy Jeff and the Fresh Prince, he had won the first Grammy ever given to a rap artist at the 31st show. "But the Grammys, they weren't televising the rap portion, you know, so we boycotted," he said. Three years later, the pair won another Grammy, but didn't think they had a chance, so they didn't attend. He then spoke movingly about

Left page from top: *Aretha Franklin • Bob Dylan*
This page: *Will Smith*

181

feeling disconnected from the music during "the rap dark ages" a few years earlier, but that artists like Tupac Shakur and the Notorious B.I.G. had inspired him to make music again. After threatening to give the speeches from the shows he had missed, Smith then dedicated this Grammy victory to the late rappers' memories and said their deaths had reminded him and other artists that they "have a responsibility … for what goes into the impressionable ears of the people listening to the music we make."

Other performance highlights included everything from a crowd-pleasing medley of *Rumours* hits from Fleetwood Mac—the album had been named Album of the Year exactly 20 years earlier—to Wyclef Jean and Erykah Badu powerfully merging his "Gone Till November" and her "On & On" (which won Best Female R&B Vocal Performance). R. Kelly soared performing "I Believe I Can Fly" before winning in the Best Male R&B Vocal Performance category and thanking everyone from Michael Jordan to Bugs Bunny for his big *Space Jam* hit.

After all the commotion and fun, Bob Dylan—a three-time winner on the night—had a way of bringing it all back to the music. When Sheryl Crow, Usher, and John Fogerty presented him with the night's final

award for Album of the Year, Dylan reflected back in time. "One time when I was about 16 or 17 years old, I went to see Buddy Holly play at a Duluth National Guard Armory and I was three feet away from him and he looked at me," Dylan recalled. "And I just have some kind of feeling that he was—I don't know how or why—but I know he was with us all the time when we were making this record in some kind of way. In the words of the immortal Robert Johnson, 'The stuff we got will bust your brains out.'" And on this historic night, Dylan did just that.

Finally, the 40th Annual Grammys also featured what is considered to be the greatest last-second substitution act in Grammy history. When Grammy Legend Award recipient Luciano Pavarotti's throat problems caused him to cancel his performance of "Nessun Dorma" from Puccini's opera *Turandot* just a few hours before showtime, the Grammy production team was able to get Aretha Franklin—who had sung the same piece at the MusiCares Person of the Year fundraiser two nights earlier—to step in "literally at a moment's notice," as Sting said in his introduction. Fortunately, the Queen of Soul showed a new side of her extraordinary talent to a watching world and helped save this Grammy performance.

Left page clockwise from top left: *Shawn Colvin • Fiona Apple • R. Kelly* This page: *Erykah Badu and Wyclef Jean*

# 41st Annual Grammy Awards

SHRINE AUDITORIUM, LOS ANGELES

*Eligibility Year: October 1, 1997–September 30, 1998*
*Announced on February 24, 1999*

"There are so many women nominated this year, Fox is backstage filming their own TV special—'When Divas Attack,'" host Rosie O'Donnell joked early in her first appearance as a Grammy host. In truth, this Grammy night at the Shrine Auditorium would turn out to be a big night for female artists. Most notably, Lauryn Hill won five Grammy awards—Album of the Year (a first for any hip-hop artist), Best New Artist, Best Female R&B Vocal Performance, Best Rhythm & Blues Song, and Best R&B Album—and delivered a stunning version of "To Zion" (with a little help from Carlos Santana) from *The Miseducation of Lauryn Hill*.

Hill had plenty of female company at the top of the world. Coming off a *Titanic* smash, Celine Dion won Record of the Year and Best Female Pop Vocal Performance for "My Heart Will Go On," which was also honored as Song of the Year for songwriters Will Jennings and James Horner. And Madonna, who won three awards herself during the night, opened the televised festivities with her first Grammy performance, singing "Nothing Really Matters" from her acclaimed *Ray of Light* album with a decidedly Asian look.

O'Donnell followed suit, entering along with two sushi chefs who eventually revealed themselves to have written "Soy" and "Sauce" on their chests—a sly reference to the previous year's Soy Bomb disturbance. O'Donnell then introduced Alanis Morissette's performance of "Uninvited" from the *City of Angels* soundtrack, which won Best Female Rock Vocal Performance and Best Rock Song, by saying, "Some of us take our broken, obsessive relationships to therapy, she's taken hers to number one."

Other standout performances by women included a rocking performance of "There Goes the Neighborhood" by Sheryl Crow, whose *The Globe*

Left page: *Ricky Martin*
This page: *Luciano Pavarotti*

*Sessions* then took home the award for Best Rock Album. Country diva Shania Twain, who won two awards, made a vivid impression in an ultra-sexy black outfit that didn't exactly conjure up images of the Grand Ole Opry. It was the Dixie Chicks, however, who received the award for Best Country Album for *Wide Open Spaces*, a fact that seemed to totally surprise them. "We thought for sure Shania got it," Dixie Chick Martie Maguire explained. "We're freaking out."

For the record, there were men on the show, too. In fact, for many, the 41st Annual Grammy Awards will be remembered as the night that Ricky Martin became a star in any language with a completely winning performance of "The Cup of Life." O'Donnell jokingly translated the title as "I Survived Menudo" before Martin's performance, but spoke for millions afterward when she sang his praises. Moments later, he won the award for Best Latin Pop Performance for "Vuelve."

Aerosmith—winner of Best Rock Performance by a Duo or Group with Vocal for "Pink"—performed their *Armageddon* soundtrack smash ballad "I Don't Want to Miss a Thing." Director George Lucas introduced a segment on the power of film music that featured James Horner and John Williams conducting

selections from the scores to *Titanic* and *Star Wars*, respectively. A year after his last-minute cancellation and replacement by Aretha Franklin, Luciano Pavarotti returned to offer his "Nessun Dorma" from Puccini's opera *Turandot*. And Mel Brooks and Carl Reiner brought the Shrine audience to their feet when they prevailed over Jerry Seinfeld, Steve Martin, Jeff Foxworthy, and the Firesign Theatre to win Best Spoken Comedy Album for *The 2000 Year Old Man in the Year 2000*. Of their fellow nominees, Brooks praised them as, "All good—not as good as us, but all good." Carl Reiner then explained, "Thirty-nine years ago we were nominated for [a] Grammy and didn't win. We can't wait another 39 years— they can."

Yet it was Will Smith who might have provided the biggest laugh of the Grammy night. Accepting the award for Best Rap Solo Performance for "Gettin' Jiggy Wit It," Smith explained that he had been to his first parent-teacher meeting earlier in the day, and that the teacher expressed pleasure with his young son Trey's progress … except for his rhyming skills. "That's just pure parental neglect," Smith joked. "So I want to dedicate this award to my son Trey. And Trey, there's always law school, baby."

Left page clockwise from top left: *Lauryn Hill • Shania Twain • Brian Setzer and guest* This page: *Celine Dion and Andrea Bocelli*

# 2000s

The '70s' "Me Decade" becomes the "My" generation: MySpace, reality TV, and user-generated content are the catchphrases of a shifting infotainment landscape. The iPod becomes an icon while Iraq dominates the national headlines. Perhaps rising above it all, a series of tragic events—September 11, the 2004 Indian Ocean tsunami, and the devastation that followed Hurricane Katrina in New Orleans and the Gulf Coast, as well as the Iraq war—bring a response from musicians in keeping with the long tradition of artists. Together

with those artists, the Grammys respond to these events in a variety of powerful ways, whether through the emotional return of the show to New York in 2003, the all-star version of "Across the Universe" made available as a download to support victims of the tsunami, or the rousing salute to the legacy of New Orleans at the 48th Annual Grammy Awards. As a result, the Grammys—and stars of the decade such as Christina Aguilera, Coldplay, Green Day, Norah Jones, OutKast, and Justin Timberlake—prove its vitality and validity, no matter the decade.

# 42nd Annual Grammy Awards

*Eligibility Year: October 1, 1998–September 30, 1999*
*Announced on February 23, 2000*

*The first* Grammy Awards ceremony held during the 21st century is perhaps best remembered as a supernaturally smooth evening for Carlos Santana. Remarkably, the veteran guitar great and bandleader had previously won only one Grammy—under his own name at the 31st Annual Grammy Awards for Best Rock Instrumental Performance (Orchestra, Group, or Soloist) for "Blues for Salvador." At the 42nd Annual Grammy Awards at Los Angeles' Staples Center, Santana made up for lost time, winning eight awards: Record of the Year, Album of the Year, Best Pop Performance by a Duo or Group with Vocal, Best Pop Collaboration with Vocals, Best Pop Instrumental Performance, Best Rock Performance by a Duo or Group with Vocal, Best Rock Instrumental Performance, and Best Rock Album. As if that

wasn't all quite enough, Santana's "Smooth" vocal guest Rob Thomas and Itaal Shur, who wrote the song together, took home the Grammy for Song of the Year.

When Bob Dylan and Lauryn Hill presented the Grammy for Album of the Year for *Supernatural* at the end of the night, Carlos Santana spoke up for "love, understanding, and oneness." But it was one of *Supernatural's* producers—and longtime Santana friend and mentor—Clive Davis who summed things up beautifully. "You're an inspiration to every young musician throughout the globe," Davis said of Santana. "Because when they break in they don't know how long a career cannot only last, but how long it can soar." On this night, there could be no question that Santana was soaring.

Also making headlines this night was Jennifer

*Left page: Rob Thomas and Carlos Santana*
*This page: Kid Rock*

**WINNER SNAPSHOT**
**Record of the Year**
"Smooth" • Santana featuring Rob Thomas
**Album of the Year**
*Supernatural* • Santana
**Song of the Year**
"Smooth" • Itaal Shur & Rob Thomas, songwriters
**Best New Artist**
Christina Aguilera

**SPECIAL MERIT AWARDS**
Lifetime Achievement Award
Harry Belafonte, Woody Guthrie, John Lee Hooker, Mitch Miller, Willie Nelson

Trustees Award
Clive Davis, Phil Spector

Technical Grammy Award
AMS Neve plc, Bill Putnam

Legend Award
Elton John

Lopez, whose rather minimalist green gown was much talked about. As Lopez's copresenter David Duchovny quipped onstage, "This is the first time in five or six years that I'm sure that *nobody* is looking at me."

Among the others whom the crowd at Staples was looking at: Will Smith, who opened the show, the Dixie Chicks, TLC, Kid Rock, and Britney Spears, whose performance began with a little girl watching the 32nd Annual Grammy Awards dreaming of someday performing on the show. There was also a rousing segment dedicated to the wide world of Latin music (celebrating the launch of the first Latin Grammy Awards in September of 2000), with fine performances from Marc Anthony, Poncho Sanchez, Ibrahim Ferrer of Buena Vista Social Club fame, and Ricky Martin, a year after his triumphant performance of "The Cup of Life."

But it wasn't all good vibes, revealing dresses, and cool performances at the 42nd Annual Grammy Awards. Despite, at the time, having established a reputation as "The Queen of Nice," Rosie O'Donnell had quite a barbed

turn as host this year. In particular, she took aim at Whitney Houston. The host made repeated allusions to Houston's recent arrest for marijuana possession at a Hawaiian airport, both in her opening monologue and with this introduction to the singer's performance of "It's Not Right But It's Okay": "Our next performer is a huge fan of the doobies," O'Donnell said. Houston surmounted the jabs with a soulful version of the song and a win for Best Female R&B Vocal Performance.

Perhaps more uplifting was the chance to watch one legendary piano man salute another. Billy Joel took the stage to honor Elton John, the recipient of a Grammy Legend Award. "In an age of Stratocasters and wah-wah pedals, Elton John made it cool to be a piano player," Joel explained, before Elton John performed "Philadelphia Freedom" with a little vocal support from the Backstreet Boys. "Now he is a knight, and in the United Kingdom he should be addressed as Sir Elton, but here in the good ol' USA his friends can still call him Sharon."

*Left page clockwise from top left: David Duchovny and Jennifer Lopez • Britney Spears • Will Smith This page: Christina Aguilera*

*Did You Know ...?* Kate Winslet (along with Wynton Marsalis and Graham Greene) takes home the Grammy for Best Spoken Word Album for Children for Listen to the Storyteller. • Cher wins her only Grammy, for "Believe" (Best Dance Recording). • Christina Aguilera tops Britney Spears among others for Best New Artist.

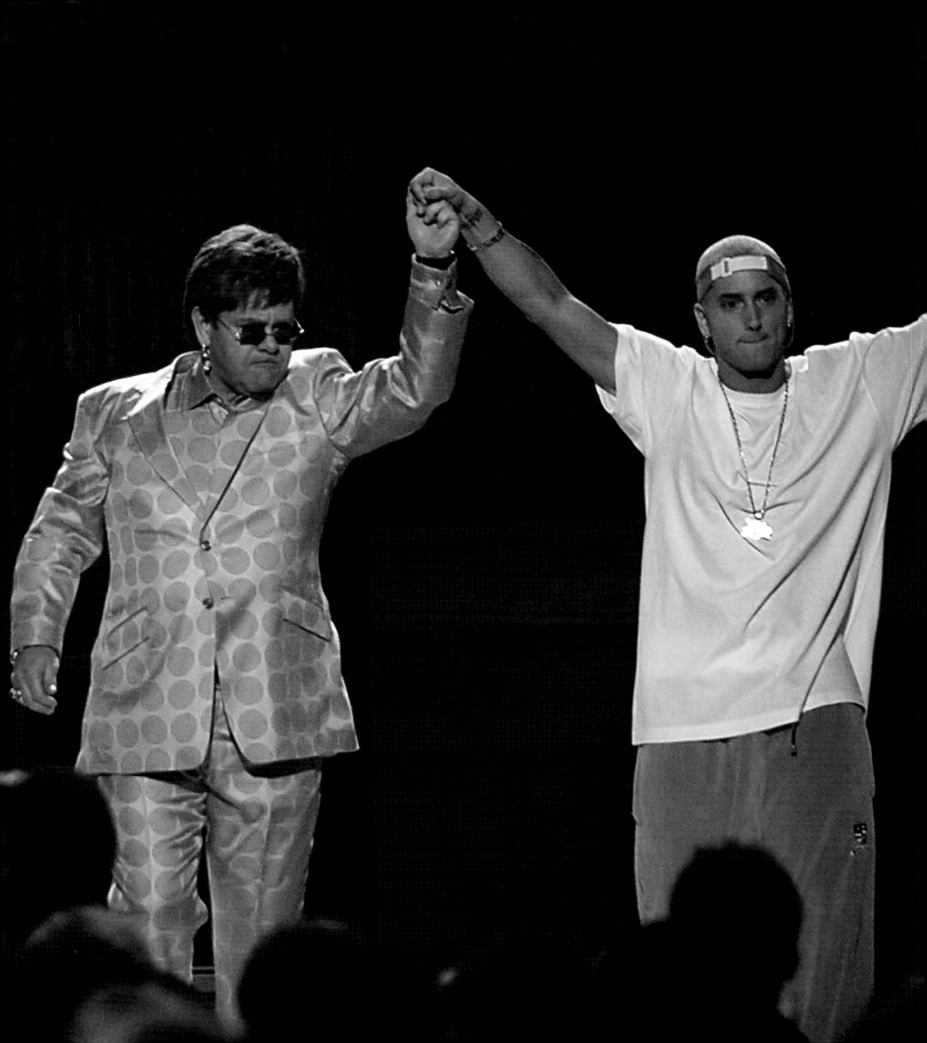

# 43rd Annual Grammy Awards

STAPLES CENTER, LOS ANGELES

*Eligibility Year: October 1, 1999–September 30, 2000*
*Announced on February 21, 2001*

"*Music makes* the people come together."

Rarely has an opening song spoken more directly to the spirit of the Grammys than Madonna's "Music," which kick-started the 43rd annual show at Los Angeles' Staples Center. Her Blondness made a big entrance onto the stage in a glittery limo driven by Lil' Bow Wow. Soon the number took a sexier turn, and, at one point, Madonna took off her leather jacket to reveal a Material Girl T-shirt and then seemed to thoroughly enjoy what is perhaps best described as a cargasm.

Host Jon Stewart established his self-deprecating tone right off, talking about how he's getting older and noting, "As I was watching Madonna writhing around on the hood of the car, all I could think was—that's *really* gonna drive up her insurance premiums."

Yet it was not Madonna providing the biggest controversy du jour on this Grammy night. Instead, the big talk of the night was Eminem, who had already

achieved tremendous commercial success, but not yet the mainstream cultural respectability that would come with the film *8 Mile* two years later. Often criticized for homophobic and sexist lyrics, Eminem made huge headlines by agreeing to perform "Stan," his edgy song about an obsessed fan, with openly gay music legend Elton John.

Stewart both commented on the tension and slyly diffused it, explaining in his monologue, "There's a tremendous amount of controversy here tonight. I think we have to deal with it right off the top. I don't know what all the controversy is about, quite frankly. I've met Eminem. I met him backstage and he's *really* gay. I mean just about the gayest guy you'd ever meet."

Before the night's most buzzed about unlikely duo took the stage, a procession of other significant stars took their turn. 'N Sync (introduced by Stewart as including two extra members, "Fredo" and "Kitten") performed an inventively lit rendition of "This

*Left page: Elton John and Eminem*
*This page: Tim McGraw and Faith Hill*

I Promise You." Sheryl Crow (who took home Best Female Rock Vocal Performance for "There Goes the Neighborhood" from *Live in Central Park*) and Shelby Lynne (who won Best New Artist) teamed up for a strong duet on Crow's "The Difficult Kind." Moby, Jill Scott, and the Blue Man Group pooled their deep talents on Moby's "Natural Blues" for one of the more beautiful and experimental Grammy performances. Destiny's Child sang "Independent Women, Part 1" and "Say My Name" for a big, sultry three-ring production number. Later, Faith Hill would perform "Breathe" in front of assorted art masterpieces looking very much like a masterpiece herself.

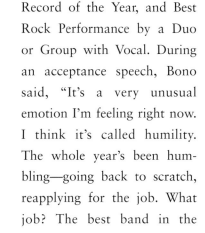

And when Eminem first took to the stage for his acceptance speech for the Best Rap Album Grammy for *The Marshall Mathers LP*, he came across as charming and uncharacteristically diplomatic. "What should I say first?" he asked openly. "I guess, first of all, I want to thank everybody who could look past the controversy or whatever and see the album for what it was … and also for what it isn't." Among the many people he thanked was his mentor Dr. Dre, who was named Producer of the Year.

"I don't know how you feel, but I was very impressed by Eminem's poise," the host noted later. "I really think this experience is gonna help him grow

as a person. As a matter of fact, after doing the duet with Elton John, I've heard that he's agreed to go to the bathroom with George Michael as well." Despite considerable laughter, Stewart then added, "Can I say something: I feel your scorn and I accept it."

There was no scorn and a few big awards for U2. The band performed a fittingly radiant version of "Beautiful Day," which was named Song of the Year, Record of the Year, and Best Rock Performance by a Duo or Group with Vocal. During an acceptance speech, Bono said, "It's a very unusual emotion I'm feeling right now. I think it's called humility. The whole year's been humbling—going back to scratch, reapplying for the job. What job? The best band in the world job." Meanwhile, it was a significantly older band who won Album of the Year: Steely Dan for their impressive comeback effort, *Two Against Nature*.

When they finally hit the stage, Eminem and Elton John didn't seem like two against nature, or even two against the world, but an unbeatable musical team. Academy President Michael Greene introduced the performance, pointing out, "We can't edit out the art that makes us uncomfortable—remember that's what our parents tried to do to Elvis, the Stones, and the Beatles." In the end, Eminem and Elton John's Grammy date with destiny was nervy, artistic, and a defining moment in Grammy history.

*Left page clockwise from top left: Toni Braxton • Madonna with Lil' Bow Wow • Destiny's Child • Macy Gray This page: Moby with the Blue Man Group*

*Did You Know …?* Boxer Oscar De La Hoya is nominated for Best Latin Pop Album for Oscar De La Hoya. *He lost to Shakira's* Shakira—MTV Unplugged. • *Elton John wins a Grammy as composer for* Elton John and Tim Rice's Aida *in Best Musical Show Album. Rice was a cowinner as lyricist along with the album's producers.* • *This is the first year for the Best Native American Music Album category. The award went to* Gathering of Nations Pow Wow, *which was produced by Tom Bee and Douglas Spotted Eagle. The award was presented on the telecast by Robbie Robertson and Val Kilmer.*

# 44th Annual Grammy Awards

STAPLES CENTER, LOS ANGELES

*Eligibility Year: October 1, 2000–September 30, 2001*
*Announced on February 27, 2002*

*The first* Grammy Awards ceremony after September 11, 2001, began on a most fitting note with a powerful performance by U2, a band whose relationship with America had only deepened in the wake of the recent tragic events. Bono and company opened the 44th Annual Grammy Awards with a characteristically heartfelt version of "Walk On," a song that, despite being written before September 11, somehow spoke to the need to press forward under even the most difficult of circumstances.

Jon Stewart—hosting for the second consecutive year at Staples Center in Los Angeles—pressed forward in his own comedic way with an entrance delayed by an onstage security check that left him standing in only his underwear and socks. "Remember when security was tight because Eminem was going to sing with Elton John?" Stewart quipped, referring to the controversial performance on the previous year's Grammy show. "Those were the days, weren't they, folks?"

The first award of the night—Best Pop Performance by a Duo or Group with Vocal—was presented by Britney Spears and *Friends* star Matthew Perry, who flirted in a good-natured way with the current teen superstar. "Matthew, this is awkward to say in front of the entire planet and all, but I guess I think of you as a 'Friend,'" she explained gently. The pair then presented the award to U2 for "Stuck in a Moment You Can't Get Out Of." Bono wryly explained that by winning a few awards, the band would now be allowed back into their native country Ireland, "So this is a public safety issue." Ultimately, U2 would win four Grammys on this night, including Record of the Year for "Walk On."

Another of the evening's most memorable performances came from the movie *Moulin Rouge.*

*Left page: Alicia Keys*
*This page: Jon Stewart*

**WINNER SNAPSHOT**
**Record of the Year**
"Walk On" • U2
**Album of the Year**
*O Brother, Where Art Thou?* Soundtrack • Various Artists
**Song of the Year**
"Fallin'" • Alicia Keys, songwriter
**Best New Artist**
Alicia Keys

**SPECIAL MERIT AWARDS**
Lifetime Achievement Award
Perry Como, Rosemary Clooney, Count Basie, Al Green, Joni Mitchell

Trustees Award
Tom Dowd, Alan Freed

Technical Grammy Award
Dr. Robert Moog, Apple Computer, Inc.

With minimal clothing and maximum soul, Christina Aguilera, Lil' Kim, Mya, and Pink then brought "Lady Marmalade" to life, assisted by the great Patti LaBelle, who performed the original hit version with her group LaBelle in 1974. Stewart responded with one of his sharpest self-deprecating lines of the night: "I come out in my underwear, you don't know what's going on. They come out, you give them a standing ovation." Stewart went on to confess, "I actually lost my virginity to that song—not the original, that version actually, a couple of months ago." The women were perhaps more excited by the fact that "Lady Marmalade" won the Grammy for Best Pop Collaboration with Vocals.

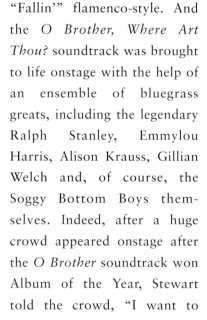

September 11, 2001, had been the planned date of the 2nd Annual Latin Grammy Awards, and time was taken to acknowledge two of the winners from a telecast that had to be cancelled—Colombian rocker Juanes, along with Spaniard Alejandro Sanz, who performed an exuberant "Quisiera Ser" with Destiny's Child.

Other notable performances included an intense rendition of "No More Drama" by Mary J. Blige, New York homeboys Tony Bennett and Billy Joel dueting on "New York State of Mind," and Bob Dylan performing "Cry a While" in what appeared to be a big white box—paradoxically, a pretty out-of-the-box idea. Equally outstanding were performances from two of the night's most notable winners. Alicia Keys—whose five awards for the evening were Song of the Year, Best New Artist, Best Female R&B Vocal Performance, Best R&B Song, and Best R&B Album (Songs in A Minor)—performed "Fallin'" flamenco-style. And the O Brother, Where Art Thou? soundtrack was brought to life onstage with the help of an ensemble of bluegrass greats, including the legendary Ralph Stanley, Emmylou Harris, Alison Krauss, Gillian Welch and, of course, the Soggy Bottom Boys themselves. Indeed, after a huge crowd appeared onstage after the O Brother soundtrack won Album of the Year, Stewart told the crowd, "I want to point out you get to come up if you worked on the album, not just if you heard it."

It was not all laughs—when country great Alan Jackson performed "Where Were You (When the World Stopped Turning)" in front of children's art created in reaction to September 11, it was in the end an emotional but ultimately heartening reminder that the world had now begun turning again, even if it would never be the same.

Left page clockwise from top left: *Nelly Furtado • Pink, Christina Aguilera, and Mya • OutKast* This page: *India.Arie*

*Did You Know ...?* India.Arie earns seven nominations, including nominations in the top four categories—Record of the Year, Album of the Year, Song of the Year, and Best New Artist—but is shut out of winning any. The following year she wins two awards.

# 45th Annual Grammy Awards

MADISON SQUARE GARDEN, NEW YORK CITY

*Eligibility Year: October 1, 2001–September 30, 2002*
*Announced on February 23, 2003*

*You could* say that the 45th Annual Grammy Awards was the first show without a single official host, but in truth the host of the show was no less a shining star than New York City itself. At the end of a frigid and snowbound winter week, a galaxy of musical stars gathered inside the Big Apple's famed Madison Square Garden to heat things up on an evening that marked the return of Music's Biggest Night to Manhattan for the first time since the tragic events of September 11. Fittingly, this emotional event would prove an altogether moving musical homecoming and arguably the city's first major positive event since the terrorist attacks.

This Grammy show began with a post-*Graduate* Dustin Hoffman introducing the first public performance of Paul Simon and Art Garfunkel in a decade. The legendary duo broke their long and sometimes tense silence by performing a stunningly lovely acoustic version of their first hit, "The Sound of Silence," standing side-by-side on a tiny circular stage. Simon & Garfunkel's moving reunion—later to be continued with a massively

successful tour—had its roots in the pair being presented with The Academy's Lifetime Achievement Award. This honor began a conversation that gradually became reconciliation—a particularly meaningful one in the wake of recent events.

These two sons of New York City weren't the only local heroes taking the stage at Madison Square Garden this special night—an impressive procession of great New Yorkers and lovers of the city from around the world joined them. For example, it was New York's own Tony Bennett and Joe Pantoliano who introduced the subtle, jazzy performance of "Don't Know Why" by Norah Jones, the woman who would own much of this notable Grammy night. "I want to tell you something about this lady," Bennett told the crowd. "She is phenomenal—she is gonna be around a long time." By the end of the night, Jones would earn five Grammys, tying Alicia Keys and Lauryn Hill for the most wins in a year ever by a female artist (Beyoncé would join this elite group the following year), while Jones' debut album, *Come Away*

**WINNER SNAPSHOT**
**Record of the Year**
"Don't Know Why" • Norah Jones
**Album of the Year**
*Come Away with Me* • Norah Jones
**Song of the Year**
"Don't Know Why" • Jesse Harris, songwriter
**Best New Artist**
Norah Jones

**SPECIAL MERIT AWARDS**
Lifetime Achievement Award
Etta James, Johnny Mathis, Glenn Miller, Tito Puente, Simon & Garfunkel

Trustees Award
Royal Blakeman, Alan Lomax, New York Philharmonic

Technical Grammy Award
Geoff Emerick, Shure Incorporated

Legend Award
The Bee Gees

*with Me*, would earn an astounding overall total of eight awards this night.

Yet, on a night when one new musical star dominated the major awards so thoroughly, there was no shortage of stellar performances. Rookie Vanessa

Carlton and Best New Artist nominee John Mayer formed a sort of singer/songwriters' circle with an artist whom Mayer rightly introduced as "the blueprint": James Taylor, who teamed with renowned cellist Yo-Yo Ma for a characteristically elegant rendition of "Sweet Baby James." Later, members of the New York Philharmonic, under the baton of David Robertson, performed an inspired version of Leonard Bernstein's "The Dance at the Gym (Mambo)" from *West Side Story*, and then joined with Coldplay for a rousing rendition of "Politik" (with the late Michael Kamen conducting). This bold and beautiful collaboration brought together—as John Leguizamo promised in his introduction—"two distinguished groups separated by a body of water but united by a shared passion for the endless possibilities of music."

Two of the emotional highlights of the night came with the help of a rock legend not from New York, but just across the Hudson in the Garden State. First, Bruce Springsteen—who won three awards during the night— and the E-Street Band performed "The Rising," his acclaimed response to the trauma of September 11. Soon after, Springsteen, Steven Van Zandt, Elvis Costello, and

Dave Grohl of the Foo Fighters—backed by No Doubt's Tony Kanal on bass and Costello cohort Pete Thomas on drums— brought the Grammys' first ever "In Memoriam" tribute to a blistering conclusion, playing the Clash's apocalyptic punk anthem "London Calling" in honor of the group's Joe Strummer, who had died just two months earlier.

Throughout this eclectic and emotional evening, respects were paid in varied ways. Accepting the Grammy for Best Rap Album (for *The Eminem Show*), Eminem took the opportunity to properly thank a long list of rap icons who had influenced him, including Run-D.M.C., the Beastie Boys, and Notorious B.I.G. Even more poignant was the presentation of a Grammy Legend Award to the Bee Gees, whose Maurice Gibb had died suddenly on January 12, and which Ed Bradley proclaimed was offered "in recognition of a lifetime of the best sort of harmony." The two surviving Brothers Gibb accepted their awards, joined by Maurice's son Adam, who accepted his father's award with great dignity. "I know how much my dad loved doing what he did," he explained, "and he would have loved being here right now. I know he'd want to thank one person and that's my mom, because she was his rock."

In the end, this moving night of music in New York City proved a fitting occasion for old friends to reunite and a true Grammy night to remember.

*Left page clockwise from top: Bruce Springsteen and Elvis Costello*
• *Coldplay's Chris Martin*
• *No Doubt's Gwen Stefani*
• *B.B. King wins two Grammy Awards, for Best Pop Instrumental Performance and Best Traditional Blues Album.*
**This page:**
*Robin Williams, Tim McGraw, and Faith Hill imitate a masterpiece backstage.*

*Did You Know ...?* Eight artists tie with five nominations each: Ashanti, Sheryl Crow, Eminem, Norah Jones, Avril Lavigne, Nelly, Raphael Saadiq, and Bruce Springsteen.

# 46th Annual Grammy Awards

STAPLES CENTER, LOS ANGELES

*Eligibility Year: October 1, 2002–September 30, 2003*
*Announced on February 8, 2004*

*Sometimes* a first performance can lead to a Second Coming.

Opening the 46th Annual Grammy Awards with the help of Beyoncé, the artist now currently known as Prince again proved himself to be a once and future musical royalty. Dressed in—what else?—purple, Prince teamed up with the recently solo Beyoncé for an inspired run-through of three songs from *Purple Rain*, which 20 years after their release retained their power to thrill with soul and style. The medley of "Purple Rain," "Baby, I'm a Star," and "Let's Go Crazy"—weaving in a taste of Beyoncé's "Crazy in Love"—featured actual pyrotechnics at the end, but there were musical fireworks right from the start. Things worked out pretty nicely for Destiny's most famous child, as well, since Beyoncé became a big winner, later giving a stunningly artistic performance of "Dangerously in Love" and ultimately taking home five Grammys for the night.

Ellen DeGeneres—one of many notable presenters

during this host-less show—set the stage for a performance inspired by a significant musical anniversary. "On this night 40 years ago, the Beatles walked on the stage at the Ed Sullivan Theater and started a cultural revolution," said DeGeneres of the Fab Four's famed *Ed Sullivan Show* appearance. To honor the Beatles' singular legacy, Sting, Dave Matthews, Pharrell Williams, and Vince Gill came together to perform "I Saw Her Standing There." Later, DeGeneres returned to honor the group with The Academy's President's Merit Award and introduce George Harrison's widow Olivia Harrison and Yoko Ono, as well as taped comments from Paul McCartney and Ringo Starr.

It wasn't, however, all peace, love, and sweet nostalgia at the 46th Annual Grammy Awards. The show took place just a week after Janet Jackson's controversial Super Bowl half-time appearance, and that "wardrobe malfunction" controversy ran over into the Grammys. In the end, Jackson—booked to

**Left page:** *Beyoncé and Prince*
**This page:** *Sting and Dave Matthews rehearse backstage*

**WINNER SNAPSHOT**
**Record of the Year**
"Clocks" • Coldplay
**Album of the Year**
*Speakerboxxx/The Love Below* • OutKast
**Song of the Year**
"Dance with My Father" • Richard Marx & Luther Vandross, songwriters
**Best New Artist**
Evanescence

introduce the show's Luther Vandross salute by Alicia Keys and Celine Dion—chose not to appear. Her Super Bowl partner Justin Timberlake did appear—performing a rousing version of his "Señorita" with jazz great Arturo Sandoval, joining the Black Eyed Peas for "Where Is the Love," and winning two awards: Best Pop Vocal Album and Best Male Pop Vocal Performance. There was some further controversy when new rap icon 50 Cent seemed to protest his loss to Evanescence in the Best New Artist category by walking onto the stage anyway as they accepted their award.

President Neil Portnow, who had forcefully led The Academy through some tense moments with the network following the Super Bowl controversy, addressed the need for increased arts funding and spoke of the state of the music industry in his comments. Introducing The Academy's new What's The Download legal downloading public service initiative, Portnow proclaimed, "Our industry will emerge from what has been a perfect storm and we will reinvent and renew that which requires change."

Among the most perfect performances of the night were Best Rock Album winners the Foo Fighters and jazz keyboardist Chick Corea performing the band's "Times Like These" with some gorgeous jazzy textures;

the White Stripes whipping up "Seven Nation Army" from the Best Alternative Music Album *Elephant*; and a performance that featured Jackson Browne, Emmylou Harris, Dwight Yoakam, and Billy Bob Thornton in a touching farewell to the late great Warren Zevon that capped the in memoriam segment. Zevon had passed away in September shortly after the release of his final album, *The Wind*, which took home two Grammys. Then there was the taped message from an ailing Luther Vandross, who found the strength to send out a little "Power of Love" as only he could on a night that brought him four Grammys, including Song of the Year for "Dance with My Father," which he wrote with Richard Marx.

But on this night, no single performance could compare to one of the Grammys' most ambitious and, yes, funky musical endeavors ever: an extraordinary salute to funk officiated by "Minister Samuel L." Jackson and featuring Earth, Wind & Fire, OutKast (three-time winners on the night), Robert Randolph and the Family Band, and George Clinton and Parliament/Funkadelic. Along with OutKast's *Speakerboxxx/The Love Below* becoming the first rap album to ever win Album of the Year at the end of the night, this rousing funk medley offered proof that we can still be one nation—even perhaps one world—under a groove.

Left page clockwise from top left: *Martina McBride • Fergie of the Black Eyed Peas • Christina Aguilera • OutKast* This page: *The White Stripes*

STAPLES CENTER, LOS ANGELES

*Eligibility Year: October 1, 2003–September 30, 2004*
*Announced on February 13, 2005*

The 47th Annual Grammy Awards featured a Queen as host, but in the end it was a late great Genius who dominated the proceedings, as Ray Charles' posthumous duets album, *Genius Loves Company*, won a grand total of eight awards.

The night at Staples Center in Los Angeles began with its very own live Grammy mash-up—a massive group effort that started, logically enough, with the Black Eyed Peas' "Let's Get It Started," and went on to feature Gwen Stefani with Eve performing "Rich Girl," Los Lonely Boys singing "Heaven," Franz Ferdinand playing "Take Me Out," and Maroon5 (who later won Best New Artist) performing "This Love." This represented, as host Queen Latifah announced in the introduction, "Four stages, five bands, and 13 nominations, and that's just the opening number."

This was a big start to perhaps Music's Biggest Night ever—a wide-ranging night that included an all-star version of "Across the Universe" to raise funds for victims of the 2004 Indian Ocean tsunami with Stevie Wonder, Bono, Billie Joe Armstrong, Alicia Keys, Steven Tyler,

Norah Jones, Tim McGraw, Brian Wilson, and Alison Krauss backed by Velvet Revolver; the emotional return of a bald and beautiful Melissa Etheridge, fresh from chemotherapy treatments for breast cancer, joining Joss Stone to offer up the performance of a lifetime by singing "Piece of My Heart" in tribute to Lifetime Achievement Award recipient Janis Joplin; and a soul-sanctifying gospel sequence that saw Mavis Staples (whose family, the Staple Singers, also were honored with a Lifetime Achievement Award), John Legend, Kanye West, and the Blind Boys of Alabama take a watching world to church by way of "I'll Take You There," "Jesus Walks," and "I'll Fly Away."

Yet following his death on June 10, 2004, Ray Charles in many ways became the focus of this Grammy show. After performing her own "If I Ain't Got You," Alicia Keys welcomed to the stage Quincy Jones and Jamie Foxx, the actor and singer who gave an Oscar-winning performance as Charles in the 2004 film *Ray*. "For an old friend," Foxx explained simply before he and Keys launched into a

**WINNER SNAPSHOT**
**Record of the Year**
"Here We Go Again" • Ray Charles & Norah Jones
**Album of the Year**
*Genius Loves Company* • Ray Charles & Various Artists
**Song of the Year**
"Daughters" • John Mayer, songwriter
**Best New Artist**
Maroon5

**SPECIAL MERIT AWARDS**
Lifetime Achievement Award
Eddy Arnold, Art Blakey, Carter Family, Morton Gould, Janis Joplin, Led Zeppelin, Jerry Lee Lewis, Jelly Roll Morton, Pinetop Perkins, Staple Singers

Trustees Award
Hoagy Carmichael, Don Cornelius, Alfred Lion, Billy Taylor

Technical Grammy Award
JBL Professional, Phil Ramone

gorgeous rendition of "Georgia on My Mind" that went from mournful to joyous, with Ray Charles' longtime friend Jones conducting the orchestra behind them.

All throughout this Grammy night, there was a sense of the past and present meeting up and paying each other proper respects. After Queen Latifah helped honor rock forefather Jerry Lee Lewis as a new Grammy Lifetime Achievement Award recipient, she announced, "If rock and roll has its fathers, then here are the sons, the one, the only, U2." The Irish band had intended to perform the roof-rattling "Vertigo," but due to back problems, Bono, and the band, switched to the less familiar but more emotional "Sometimes You Can't Make It on Your Own." Turning a setback into a different moment of triumph, Bono introduced the song by saying, "This is for my father, Bob. He was a postal clerk. He would sing opera in the night in a beautiful tenor voice. I like to think when he passed away that he gave that to me. I wish I'd got to know him better."

The evening's multigenerational theme continued immediately after when Green Day were presented with the Best Rock Album award. "We know rock and roll can be dangerous and fun at the same time, so thanks a lot," Billie Joe Armstrong said in accepting the award. Later Green Day would prove this point powerfully onstage, performing an edgy and entertaining version of "American Idiot."

Other high points included a suitably Southern-fried Southern rock salute, introduced by Matthew McConaughey, with Gretchen Wilson, Keith Urban, and Tim McGraw teaming up with some Southern rock greats, including the current-day Lynyrd Skynyrd; as well as a much-discussed duet ("Escapémonos") in Spanish from Jennifer Lopez and Marc Anthony. Emerging superstar Kanye West brought the house down not just with his spirited performance, which ended with him in angel wings, but also with his acceptance speech for Best Rap Album (*The College Dropout*). "I plan to celebrate and scream and pop champagne every chance I get, because I'm at the Grammys, baby!" A clearly elated West went on to slyly say, "Everybody wanted to know what I would do if I didn't win. I guess we'll never know."

The night also featured the final Grammy appearance of James Brown, when the Godfather of Soul seemed to pass at least part of his long-burning torch by appearing—still in fine form—with Usher for a medley of "Caught Up" and part of Brown's "Sex Machine."

By evening's end, *Genius Loves Company* would take home the Album of the Year award, and Bonnie Raitt and Billy Preston would salute Charles one last time with "Do I Ever Cross Your Mind." As Recording Academy President Neil Portnow rightly pointed out in his speech, "On Music's Biggest Night, we've shown you music's true heart and soul."

*Left page clockwise from top left: Billie Joe Armstrong of Green Day • Usher and James Brown • Melissa Etheridge and Joss Stone • Keith Urban This page: Velvet Revolver*

*Did You Know ...?* *After 12 career nominations, Rod Stewart gets his first Grammy win with* Stardust—The Great American Songbook *in Best Traditional Pop Vocal Album. • After nine career nominations, Steve Earle joins him as a first-time winner for* The Revolution Starts ... Now *in Best Contemporary Folk Album.*

# 48th Annual Grammy Awards

STAPLES CENTER, LOS ANGELES

*Eligibility Year: October 1, 2004–September 30, 2005*
*Announced on February 8, 2006*

The 48th Annual Grammy Awards kicked off with one of the show's most animated opening performances ever. The imaginary cartoon band Gorillaz and the legendary superstar Madonna engaged in a high-tech collaboration that mashed up the former's global smash "Feel Good Inc." featuring De La Soul and the latter's resurgent retro hit "Hung Up," all to fine and altogether funky effect.

Alicia Keys and Stevie Wonder then took the stage as the first presenters at this host-less Grammy show, using a lower-tech approach to soulfully set up the first Grammy Awards since the destruction of the Gulf Coast by Hurricane Katrina. "We can't ignore that the past year has been a hard one for a lot of people including our friends from New Orleans—that most musical city—and the Gulf Coast," Keys noted before she and Wonder reminded a watching world of music's ability to lift us up to "Higher Ground." This dynamic duo got the Staples Center crowd singing and clapping along to an a

cappella version of "Higher Ground" that Wonder also dedicated to "the first lady of civil rights" Coretta Scott King, who died just days before the Grammy ceremony.

The pair then presented the first award of the evening for Best Female Pop Vocal Performance ("Since U Been Gone") to Kelly Clarkson, whose later performance was introduced by a clip of her speaking of her dream to someday sing on the Grammys—an inspiring self-introduction on a night that featured a few such moments. Bono, for example, set up U2's performance this way: "U2 is not a rock band really. I think it's like we're a folk band or something— the loudest folk band in the world. But once in a while there arrives a song like 'Vertigo' that makes you want to burn your house to the ground."

Indeed, U2 were burning brightly throughout this stunning Grammy night—winning five awards, including Album of the Year and Best Rock Album (*How to Dismantle an Atomic Bomb*), and Song of the

*Left page: Mary J. Blige and Bono*
*This page: Kelly Clarkson*

---

**WINNER SNAPSHOT**
**Record of the Year**
"Boulevard of Broken Dreams" • Green Day
**Album of the Year**
*How to Dismantle an Atomic Bomb* • U2
**Song of the Year**
"Sometimes You Can't Make It on Your Own" • U2, songwriters
**Best New Artist**
John Legend

215

Year ("Sometimes You Can't Make It on Your Own"). "Being in a rock band is like running away with the circus, except you always think you're gonna be the ringmaster," Bono explained at one point. "You don't expect that on more than a few occasions you may end up being the clown, the freak. But even that's okay because you're in show business."

One of the other notable winners on this Grammy night was Mariah Carey, who won three Grammys, her first in 15 years. Yet this was one of those nights when all the talk was not about the awards. Wittily and fittingly introduced by comedian Dave Chappelle in one of his first appearances on TV since famously leaving his beloved *Comedy Central* series ("Folks, the only thing harder than leaving show business is coming back"), the famously reclusive Sly Stone returned to show business, albeit briefly, at the end of a musical salute to his extraordinarily soulful music with the Family Stone that featured members of the original band, along with Steven Tyler, Joe Perry, Best New Artist John Legend, Joss Stone, Ciara, Maroon5, and many other admirers.

Ellen DeGeneres, meanwhile, offered one of the most honest and minimal introductions in Grammy history, stating, "Our next performer needs no introduction," before leaving the stage as Paul McCartney

launched into a rousing rendition of "Fine Line" from his nominated *Chaos and Creation in the Backyard* album. McCartney then explained this was his first Grammy performance and, referring to a famous John Lennon line, now that he had "passed the audition," he'd like to rock a little, before offering a blistering take on the Beatles classic "Helter Skelter." McCartney would later return to provide a brilliantly multigenerational highlight of the show when he joined Jay-Z and Linkin Park to mash up his classic "Yesterday" with "Numb/Encore" for a classic moment of Grammy musical harmony.

After many other highlights—including Kanye West and Jamie Foxx showing lots of cool old-school spirit in a big production number of "Gold Digger"—the show ended with a tribute to the sound and spirit of New Orleans. First, Recording Academy President Neil Portnow acknowledged the quick response of MusiCares in offering financial aid in the Gulf Coast. "Go to New Orleans," Portnow declared before such Crescent City greats as Allen Toussaint, Irma Thomas, and Dr. John took the stage, along with The Edge, Elvis Costello, Yolanda Adams, and Bonnie Raitt, among others. Then they were joined by Sam Moore and Bruce Springsteen to salute the late great Wilson Pickett with the nearly fitting "In the Midnight Hour," a stirring ending to a night of great soul and substance.

Left page clockwise from top left: *Madonna • John Legend • Mariah Carey • Jay-Z, Paul McCartney, and Chester Bennington of Linkin Park* This page: *Sly Stone*

# 49th Annual Grammy Awards

STAPLES CENTER, LOS ANGELES

*Eligibility Year: October 1, 2005–September 30, 2006*
*Announced on February 11, 2007*

*As the* Grammy Awards approached the Big 5-O, Music's Biggest Night rarely seemed more culturally relevant in a number of fascinating ways. First and foremost, the 49th Annual Grammy Awards proved to be a politically charged moment of truth for the Dixie Chicks. Indeed, the Chicks have long been Grammy voter favorites, but with the popularity of the war in Iraq in steep decline, the three prominent, on-air Grammy wins by the Dixie Chicks were also seen as a statement beyond merely saluting the musical excellence of Natalie Maines, Martie Maguire, and Emily Robison. As Jeff Leeds and Lorne Manly reported in the *New York Times* the next day under the headline "Defiant Dixie Chicks Are Big Winners at the Grammys": "After death threats, boycotts and a cold shoulder from the country music establishment, the Dixie Chicks gained sweet vindication Sunday night at the 49th Annual Grammy Awards, capturing honors in all five of the categories in which they were nominated."

In the wake of Maines' spontaneous 2003 antiwar remark to a London audience ("Just so you know, we're ashamed the president of the United States is from Texas."), the Dixie Chicks found themselves at the center of a tremendous firestorm—one that would seemingly end up burning many

bridges between the group and their relationship with country music radio, their longtime musical base. By the end of this Grammy night, the Dixie Chicks would surprise many observers—and by the looks on their faces, themselves as well—by taking home Grammy Awards for Record of the Year, Album of the Year, and Song of the Year, as well as Best Country Album and Best Country Performance by a Duo or Group with Vocal.

Meanwhile, in another nod to the currency of the times, the 49th awards, acknowledging the growing popularity of user-influenced media, also responded to the realities of the world around it in a far less political way with the first-ever inclusion of the "My Grammy Moment" segment, in which viewers voted to decide which of three unsigned artists would get the chance to sing live during the Grammy telecast with Justin Timberlake. Ultimately, Robyn Troup, 18, from Houston, Texas, would prevail and perform an impressive medley of Bill Withers "Ain't No Sunshine" and Timberlake's "My Love," for which she and Timberlake were joined by rap sensation T.I. Interestingly, Troup's victory was announced by *Dreamgirls* Academy Award-nominee (and, within weeks, winner) Jennifer Hudson, a former *American Idol* contestant, who declared, "I

*Left page: Mary J. Blige*
*This page: Justin Timberlake*

**WINNER SNAPSHOT**

**Record of the Year**
"Not Ready to Make Nice" • Dixie Chicks

**Album of the Year**
*Taking the Long Way* • Dixie Chicks

**Song of the Year**
"Not Ready to Make Nice" • Martie Maguire, Natalie Maines, Emily Robison & Dan Wilson, songwriters

**Best New Artist**
Carrie Underwood

**SPECIAL MERIT AWARDS**

**Lifetime Achievement Award**
Joan Baez, Booker T. and the MG's, Maria Callas, Ornette Coleman, The Doors, Grateful Dead, Bob Wills

**Trustees Award**
Estelle Axton, Cosimo Matassa, Stephen Sondheim

**Technical Grammy Award**
David M. Smith, Yamaha Corporation

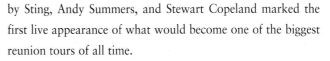
know what it's like to compete to win the chance of a lifetime."

There were, of course, many other big winners on this hot Grammy night. The Red Hot Chili Peppers won four awards and gave the final performance of the night with "Snow" from their *Stadium Arcadium* album surrounded by the biggest faux indoor snowstorm in Grammy history. Mary J. Blige won three awards, for Best R&B Album, Best R&B Song, and Best Female R&B Vocal Performance, and gave one of the longest and most emotional Grammy acceptance speeches in memory.

Other notable winners included both Timberlake and T.I., who won for Best Rap/Sung Collaboration for "My Love." Timberlake also won for Best Dance Recording for "Sexy Back," while T.I. won for Best Rap Solo Performance for "What You Know." A more senior Grammy victory was enjoyed by the great Tony Bennett—loudly saluted on air by his enthusiastic copresenter Quentin Tarantino—who won Best Pop Collaboration with Vocals for his duet with Stevie Wonder on "For Once in My Life." Not bad at all for a legendary artist who at age 80 was old enough to have also performed on the Grammy's very first "The Best on Record" telecast back in 1963. That was 20 years before the birth of country sensation Carrie Underwood, who took home the Best Female Country Vocal Performance and Best New Artist Grammys, the latter presented to her by Natalie Cole and new Lifetime Achievement honoree Ornette Coleman.

This Grammy show also helped launch one of the highest profile comebacks in pop music history when the reunited Police opened the night with "Roxanne," the very hit that launched their career some 30 years earlier. The performance

by Sting, Andy Summers, and Stewart Copeland marked the first live appearance of what would become one of the biggest reunion tours of all time.

Exciting in a different way was Colombian superstar Shakira, who made her first-ever Grammy appearance despite running a high fever. Her electrifying performance with Wyclef Jean proved the enduring truth behind the title of their smash duet "Hips Don't Lie."

And, in a segment that looked back on the rich history of seductive R&B and featured Smokey Robinson, Lionel Richie, and Chris Brown, Christina Aguilera brought down the house with an otherworldly version of "It's a Man's Man's Man's World" in tribute to the recently deceased James Brown.

More restrained but exceedingly powerful was a soulful and musically collaborative medley in which Corinne Bailey Rae, John Legend, and John Mayer came together to sing and play on each other's compositions—vivid proof, as Stevie Wonder suggested in his introduction, that anyone who thinks "they don't make singer/songwriters like they used to" ought to think again.

Finally, though, the Grammy Awards appeared to be looking energetically forward at a very healthy 49 years young, using the strength of its position as Music's Biggest Night to continue to advocate for a healthier music future. As President Neil Portnow, arguing for stronger music education and its long-term impact on the development of young musicians, said, "The time is now to contact your elected leaders. Tell them that music is just as essential to the next generation's development as any other subject … Together let us all ensure that music stays just as vital and alive for generations still to come."

Left page clockwise from top left: *The Police* • *Shakira and Wyclef Jean* • *Dixie Chicks* This page: *Carrie Underwood*

*Did You Know …?* Bon Jovi (with Jennifer Nettles on "Who Says You Can't Go Home" in Best Country Collaboration with Vocals) and Peter Frampton (for Fingerprints in Best Pop Instrumental Album) win their first-ever Grammy Awards. • President Jimmy Carter wins Best Spoken Word Album for Our Endangered Values: America's Moral Crises (in a tie with Ossie Davis and Ruby Dee's With Ossie and Ruby: In This Life Together). • Actor Joaquin Phoenix wins for his performance on the soundtrack album of the Johnny Cash biopic Walk the Line in Best Compilation Soundtrack Album for Motion Picture, Television, or Other Visual Media. T-Bone Burnett wins as album producer.

# The Recording Academy

The idea to create a Recording Academy began in early 1957 when five top Los Angeles record executives met at the request of the Hollywood Beautification Committee, which had asked them to suggest performers who deserved stars on the sidewalk of Hollywood Boulevard. From that meeting, the five-man nucleus, consisting of Paul Weston of Columbia, Lloyd Dunn of Capitol, Sonny Burke of Decca, Jesse Kaye of MGM, and Dennis Farnon of RCA Victor, along with former Columbia Records President Jim Conkling, began to explore the idea of creating an association for recording professionals that would reward artistic creativity, foster better relationships among members of the industry, and obtain world recognition.

After several discussions, the National Academy of Recording Arts & Sciences Inc. was born on May 28, 1957, at a meeting at Hollywood's legendary Brown Derby Restaurant. The first membership meeting was held almost a month later, also at the Brown Derby. Early members of The Academy's first chapter in Los Angeles included Benny Carter, Rosemary Clooney, Nat "King" Cole, Doris Day, Stan Kenton, Henry Mancini, Gisele McKenzie, and Nelson Riddle.

Soon, in preparation for bestowing awards for the best recordings, the nascent Academy actually took it upon itself to define a recording, which more than anything proves legal language is timeless:

*"Recording, as defined specifically by the National Academy of Recording Arts & Sciences: Any method, now known or unknown, by which sound is recorded, transcribed or transmitted, such sound to be preserved on tape, disc or other media now known or unknown, and placed on sale to the public within the United States and/or its*

This page: *Nat "King" Cole, Capitol Records VP Lloyd Dunn, Capitol A&R man Lee Gillette, and Academy acting national Chairman Jim Conkling at an early Academy meeting*

*possessions for home and private entertainment, said recording to include all acceptable methods now established or to be established by the phonograph recording industry such as electrical transfer of sound originally recorded on film or tape for motion pictures, transfer of sound from so-called transcription or tape originally created for radio and/or TV broadcast, or live transfer of sound from radio and/or TV."*

In 1958, then Capitol Records art director Marvin Schwartz finalized the Grammy Award design, which was then physically crafted by hand by Bob Graves. As of this writing, only one other artisan, John Billings, who apprenticed under Graves, has made the Grammy Award statue.

The record industry had apparently already established a renegade reputation for its iconoclastic approach to business; enough so to elicit the *Hollywood Reporter*'s comments on the initial Grammy Awards presentation, noting the awards' potential to become a unifying force: "[It] was the first time rival elements in one of the most competitive facets of the entire entertainment business joined together in a common enterprise designed to upgrade and add dignity to their industry."

It was followed by this now prophetic understatement: "… It seems the inaugural event bodes a likely continuance and even expansion of the Grammy Awards."

Soon, additional Academy chapters began springing up across the country, first in New York (1958), then Chicago (1961), Nashville (1964), and Atlanta (1969). Today, The Academy stands 12 chapters strong, adding, in order of formation, the Memphis, San Francisco, Texas, Philadelphia, Florida, Washington, D.C., and Pacific Northwest chapters.

Over the years, The Academy has developed additional forms of recognition alongside the iconic Grammy Award, creating Special Merit Awards to acknowledge essential musical contributions that don't fall under the umbrella of the Grammy categories. The Lifetime Achievement Award was established to recognize those who have made creative contributions of outstanding artistic significance; the Trustees Award is presented to those who have made significant contributions, other than performance, to the field of recording; the Grammy Legend Award has been presented only on occasion and is intended to recognize individuals or groups for ongoing contributions and influence in the music community; the Technical Grammy Award goes to outstanding creative audio specialists like producers and engineers as well as important corporations that have advanced the development of audio technology; and the Grammy Hall of Fame inducts recordings at least 25 years old that have shown remarkably lasting cultural value.

In 1995, The Academy launched Grammy.com with a "cybercast" of the backstage press area at the 37th Grammy Awards show. Grammy.com now stands as a robust online destination for millions of Grammy fans worldwide, industry professionals, and members of The Academy.

In 1998, The Academy established an office in the nation's capital, and today the Advocacy & Government Relations office represents artists, songwriters, studio professionals, and other music makers on matters that impact the arts and their livelihood before Congress. This is political rock in the best sense as The Academy works to protect creators' rights on a number of topics such as intellectual property rights, music preservation, music education, freedom of expression, radio reform, and other issues.

In 2000, the Producers & Engineers Wing was established as a national membership division of The Academy for producers, engineers, remixers, manufacturers, technologists, and other related creative and technical professionals in the recording community. Currently, 6,000 professionals comprise the P&E Wing, forming an organized voice for the creative and technical recording community addressing issues that affect the craft of recorded music, while ensuring its role in the development of new technologies, recording and mastering recommendations, and archiving and preservation initiatives.

In 2006, The Academy launched the Grammy University Network to engage and educate college students who are planning a career in the music or recording industry. The goal of Grammy U is to give a network of students who are currently attending colleges, universities, and technical schools access to recording industry professionals to provide a unique "out of classroom" perspective on the industry.

Today, The Academy services 18,000 members with the help of more than 175 full-time employees across the country, and the Grammy Awards have become the defining mark of excellence for music makers. All 18,000 members are involved in some manner in the recording industry or music community, including chart-topping artists, music educators and students, managers, and independent musicians. The Academy's 12,000 voting members—who cast their votes for each year's Grammy recipients—are the performers, artists, songwriters, musicians, producers, engineers, mixers, and others whose profession is making music. This is what makes the Grammy the most prestigious honor in music—and the recording industry's only peer-to-peer award.

Though fans worldwide know the Grammy Awards as the definitive music awards broadcast, The Academy, now a powerful force in music for a half-century, plays a pivotal role in the lives of musicians year-round.

## Caring for Music People

The nonprofit MusiCares Foundation was established in 1989 by The Recording Academy to provide a safety net of critical assistance for music people in times of need.

MusiCares focuses the resources and attention of the music industry on human service issues that directly impact the health and welfare of the music community. Through the years, MusiCares has helped thousands in the music industry deal with issues of substance abuse, financial crises, and other human service needs.

MusiCares also responded to the Gulf Coast hurricane tragedies of 2005 by creating the MusiCares Hurricane Relief Fund. The Fund has provided more than $4 million in financial assistance for basic needs such as food, clothing, gasoline, transportation, and medications, as well as instruments and other supplies to nearly 3,500 individuals directly affected by the disasters.

## Supporting Music Education and Preservation

The Grammy Foundation was established by The Recording Academy in 1989 to cultivate the understanding, appreciation, and advancement of the contribution of recorded music to American culture.

The Foundation accomplishes this mission through programs and activities designed to engage the music industry and cultural community as well as the general public. The Foundation works in partnership with The Recording Academy to bring national attention to important issues such as the value and impact of music and arts education and the urgency of preserving our rich cultural legacy.

In 1988, just prior to the formation of the Foundation, The Academy staged its first Grammy

### MusiCares Person of the Year

*In 1991, MusiCares presented its first Person of the Year dinner and tribute concert honoring David Crosby. Over the years, this invitation-only industry fund-raising event has honored such mega-stars as Tony Bennett, Bono, Elton John, Luciano Pavarotti, Bonnie Raitt, and Sting, and has been attended by a U.S. president and foreign royalty.*

Bono accepts his MusiCares Person of the Year honor at an evening of tribute performances in New York in 2003.

Career Day with the late salsa great Tito Puente in New York City. The event gave local area students the opportunity to talk with and ask questions of Puente to learn how a superstar artist dreamed about, pursued, and eventually achieved his career goals.

Since then, under the banner of Grammy in the Schools, the Foundation's education programs have been expanded and are now produced nationwide throughout the year. Hundreds of thousands of students have participated in these programs, whether it is a few hours spent with artists at a Grammy SoundChecks event or multiple weeks of immersive training in the "real-world" music creation, recording, and performance setting of Grammy Camp.

The Grammy Foundation's preservation and advancement initiatives are designed to support projects that increase the understanding of music and its role in society and raise public awareness of the imperiled state of our nation's recorded sound archives. The Grammy Living Histories program preserves on visual media the life stories of key recording industry luminaries such as Atlantic Records founder Ahmet Ertegun, famed piano maker Henry Steinway, B.B. King, and others who helped create recorded musical history. And since its inception, the Foundation's Grant Program has provided more than $4.5 million to individuals and organizations to preserve and catalogue individual recorded sound collections for future generations.

## Grammys on the Hill

"Protest" songs are one thing, but getting artists to participate in the political process for their own well-being has been a greater challenge. But today, making a living as a musician is more complex than ever, and legislation regulating copyright in the digital age can have a huge impact on the everyday musician.

One groundbreaking step toward achieving The Academy's advocacy goals and involving artists was the creation of Recording Arts Day on Capitol Hill, an opportunity for creative artists to meet with national leaders in Washington, D.C., and to communicate their issues on a one-on-one basis. That evening, The Academy produces its Grammys on the Hill Awards Dinner, at which legislators, educators, and artists are recognized for their contributions to the creative community. Honorees have included political leaders as well as artists such as Kelly Clarkson, Missy Elliott, Gloria Estefan, and Martina McBride.

*This page: Singer Kelly Clarkson with members of Congress at Recording Arts Day on Capitol Hill in 2006. Pictured (left to right): Reps. Joe Crowley, Connie Mack, and Mary Bono; Clarkson; Reps. Steny Hoyer, Stephanie Herseth, Marsha Blackburn, and Charles Gonzalez.*

# A Special Thanks To...

*Tony* Bennett, Ted Bergmann, Melissa Blazek, Michael Caulfield, Danny Clinch, Lester Cohen, John Cossette, Pierre Cossette, Kelly Darr, Barb Dehgan, Rick Diamond, Scott Dickscheid, The Edge, Ken Ehrlich, Christine Farnon, Aretha Franklin, Steve Granitz, Herb Hemming, Meryl Ginsberg, Doug Gore, Evan Greene, Drew Hinze, Quincy Jones, Claudine Little, Nicole Loskutoff, Paul Madeira, Marina Martinez, John Mayer, Kevin Mazur, Jim McHugh, Ann Meckelborg, Frank Micelotta, Walter C. Miller, Les Moonves, Paul Murphy, Neil Portnow, Bonnie Raitt, Phil Ramone, Iman Saadat, Carlos Santana, Louise Spear, Mary Stewart, Diane Theriot, Arnold Turner, and Stevie Wonder.

Everyone at Greenberg Traurig, especially Joel Katz, Bobby Rosenbloum, Steve Sidman, and Charmaine Williams.

Everyone at The Recording Academy, Borders Group, and Ann Arbor Media Group.

All the photographers throughout the years who have documented the extraordinary history of the Grammy Awards.

*David* Wild would like to thank Ken Ehrlich for bringing him into the Grammy family; Pierre Cossette, John Cossette, Walter C. Miller and Tisha Fein and all of his colleagues on the broadcast; and at The Academy, Neil Portnow, Terry Lickona, the entire TV Committee, Christine Farnon, and especially David Konjoyan, David Grossman, Jennifer Cebra, and everyone who brought this book to life.

# Photo Credits

*We have made great efforts to trace the copyright holders of the photographs used in this publication and, when listing any such copyright-related information in this index, to accurately reflect the copyright-related information obtained.*

Fiona Apple/R. Kelly: Copyright:
Rick Diamond

Page 183
Copyright: Rick Diamond

**41st GRAMMY AWARDS**

Page 184
Frank Micelotta

Page 185
Paul Spinelli

Page 186
All photos by Kevin Mazur

Page 187
Paul Spinelli

**42nd GRAMMY AWARDS**

Pages 190-192
All photos Copyright: Rick Diamond

Page 193
Photography by Jim McHugh

**43rd GRAMMY AWARDS**

Page 194
Frank Micelotta

Page 195
Photography by Jim McHugh

Page 196
Toni Braxton: Photography by
Jim McHugh

Madonna with Lil' Bow Wow/
Destiny's Child/Macy Gray:
Frank Micelotta

Page 197
Photography by Jim McHugh

**44th GRAMMY AWARDS**

Pages 198-199
All photos by Frank Micelotta

Page 200
Nelly Furtado: K. Winter

Pink, Christina Aguilera, and Mya:
Chris Pizzello

OutKast: Frank Micelotta

Page 201
K. Winter

**45th GRAMMY AWARDS**

Page 202
Kevin Mazur

Page 203
Danny Clinch

Page 204
Bruce Springsteen and
Elvis Costello/Coldplay/
Gwen Stefani: Kevin Mazur

B.B. King: Danny Clinch

Page 205
Copyright: Rick Diamond

**46th GRAMMY AWARDS**

Page 206
Michael Caulfield/WireImage.com

Page 207
Kevin Mazur/WireImage.com

Page 208
Martina McBride/Fergie:
Michael Caulfield/WireImage.com

Christina Aguilera: Lester
Cohen/WireImage.com

OutKast: Rick Diamond/
WireImage.com

Page 209
Kevin Mazur/WireImage.com

**47th GRAMMY AWARDS**

Page 210
Lester Cohen/WireImage.com

Page 211
Danny Clinch

Page 212
Billie Joe Armstrong of Green Day/
Usher and James Brown/ Keith
Urban: Kevin Mazur/WireImage.com

Melissa Etheridge and Joss Stone:
Lester Cohen/WireImage.com

Page 213
Steve Granitz/WireImage.com

**48th GRAMMY AWARDS**

Pages 214-215
Michael Caulfield/WireImage.com

Page 216
Madonna/Jay-Z, Paul McCartney,
and Chester Bennington of Linkin
Park: Kevin Mazur/WireImage.com

John Legend: Danny Clinch

Mariah Carey: Michael Caulfield/
WireImage.com

Page 217
Kevin Mazur/WireImage.com

**49th GRAMMY AWARDS**

Page 218
Lester Cohen/WireImage.com

Page 219
Kevin Mazur/WireImage.com

Page 220
The Police/The Dixie Chicks:
Michael Caulfield/WireImage.com

Shakira and Wyclef Jean:
Lester Cohen/WireImage.com

Page 221
Steve Granitz/WireImage.com

**THE RECORDING ACADEMY**

Page 222
William Claxton/Courtesy Demont
Photo Management

Page 225
Steve Granitz/WireImage.com

Page 226
Douglas A. Sonders/WireImage.com

**ENDPAPER**

Coolio: Photography by Jim McHugh

Eric Clapton: Photography by
Jim McHugh

Kanye West: Danny Clinch

Kelly Clarkson: Michael Caulfield/
WireImage.com

Missy Elliott: Danny Clinch

Faith Hill: Photography by
Jim McHugh

Alison Krauss: Photography by
Jim McHugh

Marc Anthony: Danny Clinch

"Weird Al" Yankovic: Sam Emerson

Billie Joe Armstrong: Steve Granitz/
WireImage.com

Quincy Jones: Sam Emerson

Carrie Underwood: Steve Granitz/
WireImage.com

Al Jarreau: Sam Emerson

Alicia Keys: Photography by
Jim McHugh

# Index

*Italics indicate illustrative material.*